HOW TO MAKE

PLAY HOUSES

HOW TO MAKE

PLAY HOUSES

PETER HOLLAND

CASSELL

A CASSELL BOOK
First published in the UK 1996 by Cassell plc,
Wellington House,
125 Strand,
London WC2R 0BB

Copyright © Text and illustrations Peter Holland 1996
Designed by Andrew Shoolbred

Distributed in the United States by Sterling Publishing Co., Inc.,
387 Park Avenue South, New York, NY 10016-8810

Distributed in Australia by Capricorn Link (Australia) Pty Ltd
2/13 Carrington Road, Castle Hill, NSW 2154

British Library Cataloguing-in-Publication Data
A catalogue entry for this title is available from the British Library

ISBN 0-304-34597-0 (Hardback)
ISBN 0-7063-7534-3 (Paperback)

Typeset by Litho Link Ltd, Welshpool, Powys, Wales

Printed & bound in slovenia by Printing House DELO-Tiskarna
by arrangement with Korotan Ljubljana

Contents

Introduction

Is your garden large enough to take a traditional play-house? Perhaps your idea of a play-house is a miniature garden shed, in which your children have to pretend that it is warm in the winter and that the inside is nearer to the standard of a real room in a real house?

This book shows how play-houses can be made to take apart for convenient storage in the house or garage. They can be made small enough to be used in the playroom or children's bedroom, the garage, or when the weather is fair, outdoors in a tiny garden. Here is your chance to make some very special play-houses, complete with accessories, for your young householders: read on.

Does your child have a favourite interest or play theme? This book contains fourteen different designs for play-houses, ranging from a simple stable complete with a morris dance-type horse, to a railway station where the ticket-collector can be signalman and station-master as well.

Each of the play-houses is designed to offer the maximum theme-play facilities, in a tiny space. It can result in a package which takes up only just over a metre (40 in) square of floor space in a room, garage or patio area. Most should have enough headroom, where it matters, to accommodate children of up to nine years old. When they are not in use, most of the play-houses will fold up to lean against a wall, where they take up around 200 mm × 1 m (8 × 40 in) of floor space. They consist of sections which are hinged together and lock in place with pegs. They are quite light, and can be assembled in a few minutes.

These play-houses are not merely boxes in which to play; each project has fittings, accessories and furnishings to provide the basic encouragement for creative play. Indeed, your children may, with your guidance, be able to help with some of these later stages of construction.

You don't have to be a proficient woodworker to create the play-houses in this book. Each project is described in easy-to-follow cutting and assembly stages. The materials used are mostly thin plywood and strips of small-section pine, both of which you can buy at fairly reasonable cost at timber-yards or DIY centres. The joints are simple in the extreme, and you only need a few tools. The projects have similar methods of construction, so if you wish to make additional play-houses, there is little else to learn.

A garage is an ideal place in which to lay out each plywood sheet for marking-out and cutting. A folding workbench such as a Workmate completes the work area: a proper workshop is not essential. After reducing some of the plywood to convenient half-sheets outdoors, the projects can be completed on the floor of a spare bedroom, using a length of 51 × 76 mm (2 × 3 in) timber as a cutting and nailing support, and the Workmate for the smaller items.

Now look at the list of projects. Which of the following play themes would your children enjoy? Keeping a village store or a boutique, mending cars, owning a pony, being a brain surgeon, or a station-master? Or perhaps running a café, living in the year 2010, manning a space shuttle, or directing a TV show? How about driving a camper, or busting into a western saloon? Perhaps a little quiet work in a kitchen/diner with all mod cons, or hiding away in a two-floor tree-house (which is really indoors). It's all so much more alive than watching TV or playing a computer game!

Each project has purpose-made aids to encourage inspirational and interactive play – from simple seating to robot pet, old crock car to flame-effect cooking hobs. Those theme-related items of play can also be used separately, thus obviating the need to buy and adapt, or to make specific miniature furniture and toys.

Making a project can be both relaxing and rewarding. It can also save money and gladden young hearts – a combination not easily found these days.

Basic Tips

Although the play-houses in this book are diverse in appearance, shape and function, most of them have a similar basic construction. This chapter shows you how to hinge pieces together, reinforce edges and connect them – all basic techniques for the long list of projects. First, though, your materials.

PLYWOOD

Walls, roof and floor are all made from 4 mm ($\frac{3}{16}$ in) plywood. It is generally sold in 2438 × 1219 mm (8 × 4 ft) sheets. You can also use hardboard for some of the smaller, non-structural components.

Plywood is thin, but it is also light and if you can buy the type which has the centre lamination thicker than the outer laminations, it will be almost as rigid in each direction. Fig. 1.1 shows the difference. The outlines shown on each of the cutting diagrams ensure that, where there is a more rigid dimension, this is incorporated where it works best. After you buy the wood, store it flat on the floor in a dry place. Ideally, get to work on the panel-cutting right away, and store the parts flat until you are ready for them. Plywood will curl or warp if it is stood up against a wall, or if you collected it on a car roof-rack in wet weather. If this happens, let it dry out before you start.

Fig. 1.1

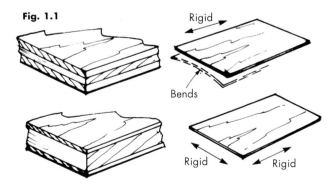

STRIP WOOD

You will find that some panels are rather flimsy in appearance where there are door and window openings. This is where a light edge framework restores rigidity.

Fig. 1.2

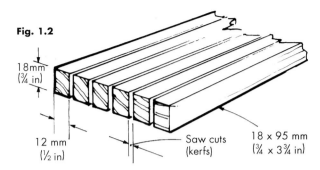

All projects use 12 × 18 mm ($\frac{1}{2}$ × $\frac{3}{4}$ in) strips of pine for this. It is available at most timber-yards or DIY centres and is usually sold by the metre. The exact dimensions of this pine are not critical. If you have a hand-held circular saw or a small saw bench, you can quickly rip 12 mm ($\frac{1}{2}$ in) strips from 18 mm ($\frac{3}{4}$ in) thick strips of wider section, or from a board (Fig. 1.2). Some of the prototypes were made in this way, recycling old pieces of pine cladding.

Edge trims to some roof panels, in the angle of some joints and as window frames, are cut from 12 mm ($\frac{1}{2}$ in) square strip (also available by the metre, in pine). Be careful, though, to avoid large

Fig. 1.3

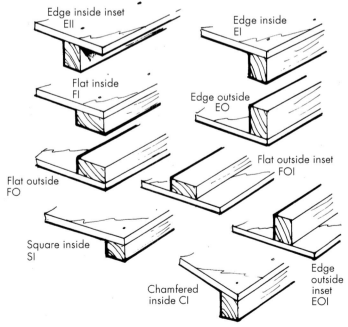

knots, and store the strips flat and dry. Fig. 1.3 shows how you position both types of strip on the panels. For the sake of clarity, and because it would be long-winded to refer to each arrangement in the project diagrams, they are referred to by letter. In a few cases you have to chamfer one edge of the strip with a plane before you fix it in place. Where wall panels are hinged together at a corner, each supports the other, obviating the need for a wood strip there.

HINGES

Now you might think that such small-section wood would not offer a good hold for screws when hinging pieces together. The play-houses have lots of hinged edges, but on most of the projects there is not a metal hinge in sight. For many years, draught screens and clothes-horses have used a special type of hinge. This type of hinge also works well for the light wall and door panels of the play-houses. These hinges are made from strips of upholstery webbing, which you can buy at needlework shops. This arrangement is quick to fix, takes up very little thickness, and is low in cost.

Fig. 1.4 shows how to position short pieces of webbing, and the fixing sequence. Start the job off with a hot-melt glue gun and its glue stick, then use a domestic iron to make a complete bond. Clean the iron carefully afterwards, to avoid domestic trouble and shiny collars!

Follow this sequence, which forms part of the stable project:

1 Always do the hinging *before* adding the edging strips. Lay the ply pieces in position, flat on the floor or on a sheet of hardboard. Hinges do not bond well if the components are upright or are not level with each other.

Cut 38 mm (1½ in) long strips of 25 mm (1 in) wide strong upholstery webbing and lay them in equally spaced pairs along the edge to be hinged.

2 Using the glue gun and woodwork-type glue sticks, put a blob of glue about the size of a drawing-pin head 12 mm (½ in) in from the edge. Quickly press one of the webbing pieces onto it so that it is midway across the joint. Be careful not to let the webbing unravel. The glue will prevent this when the hinge is complete, but the webbing is

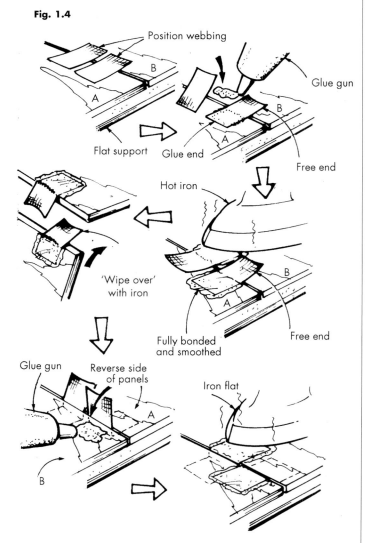

Fig. 1.4

Position webbing · Glue gun · Flat support · Glue end · Free end · B · A · Hot iron · 'Wipe over' with iron · Fully bonded and smoothed · Free end · B · A · Glue gun · Reverse side of panels · A · B · Iron flat

liable to catch on the ply edge or adjacent glue.

Continue in pairs, down the whole set of hinges. Be sure to glue them alternately to frame and door or opposite panels. They have to be almost touching each other.

3 Using the domestic iron on its hottest setting, iron over the hinges to remelt and spread the glue fully into the weave. Hold the unglued end as you wipe the iron away from the ply edge. Do the same with the other pairs – remember not to glue both ends of any hinge yet. Lift the panels clear, when they will separate. Gently pass the iron over the edge, to make each piece of webbing bend around the edge.

4 Turn both pieces of plywood over to the other face and lay them flat. Slide the edges together, when the webbing, which should be sticking up, is ready for you to fix with more glue and ironing. Be sure to check that no piece of webbing is glued back onto its own side by mistake. Any rough edges of webbing should be blended with more glue and ironed over. You can tighten any loose hinges by ironing one end and dragging the webbing tight with a piece of wood (the webbing will be hot!)

QUICK-DETACH JOINTS

All the projects consist of pairs of adjacent walls hinged together, so that from a folded-flat storage position, you swing one wall open through 90 degrees, where it will stand on its own ready for joining to the next hinged pair. Thus it can be done single-handed – see Fig. 1.5.

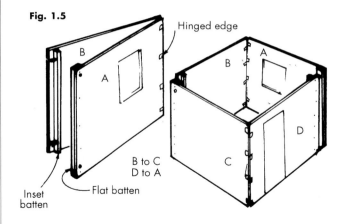

Fig. 1.5

Hinged edge

B

A

B

A

D

B to C
D to A

C

Inset batten

Flat batten

Although there are a variety of metal and plastic quick joiners to be had at DIY stores, most need the use of a screwdriver, and parts may be lost. A peg and pin joint, however, is both quick and easy to use, and does not require a spare pair of hands. This type of fastening is shown in Fig. 1.6, and is used for all the play-house projects.

You can make the peg and pin joint by drilling through two edge strips, gluing a dowel into one, and drilling the protruding end across to take a pin, which you bend with pliers from a piece of wire coat-hanger. Accessories hang on walls from hooks, which you can make from the same wire.

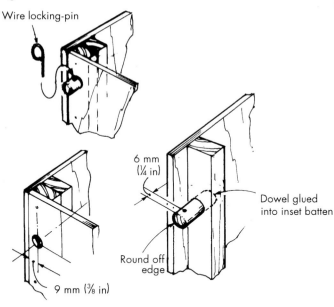

Fig. 1.6

Wire locking-pin

6 mm
(¼ in)

Dowel glued
into inset batten

Round off
edge

9 mm (⅜ in)

TOOLS

Starting with marking out, you will need the following items, shown in Fig. 1.7:

• Rule or tape
• Pencils
• Compass
• Try square
• Protractor or sliding bevel
• Marking gauge
• Marking knife

Fig. 1.7

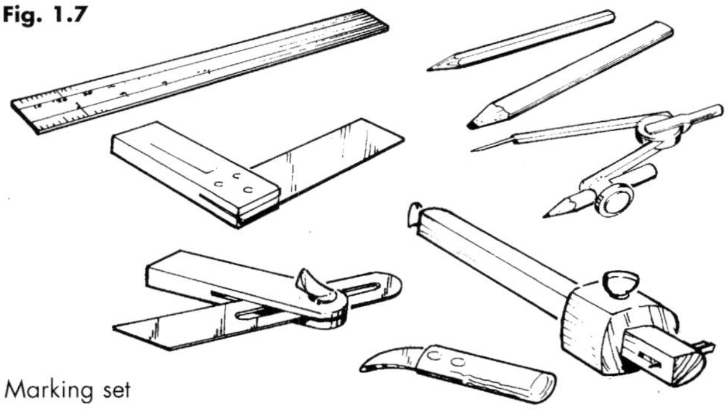

Marking set

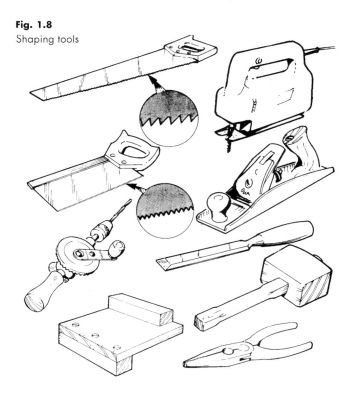

Fig. 1.8
Shaping tools

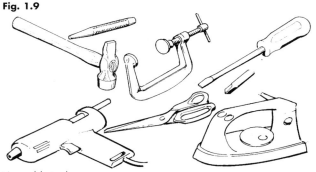

Fig. 1.9

Assembly tools

• Scissors, hot-melt glue gun and domestic iron, for fixing webbing hinges
• G-cramps
For finishing, use those tools shown in Fig. 1.10:
• Sanding block
• Filling knife
• Paint brushes

Fig. 1.10

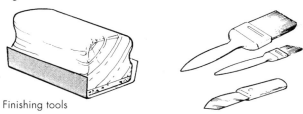

Finishing tools

OPTIONAL ITEMS

The additional items shown in Fig. 1.11 will speed the work:

Fig. 1.11

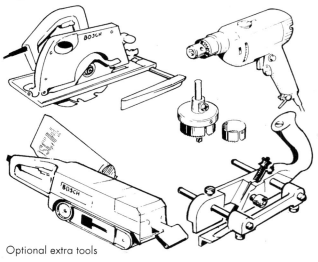

Optional extra tools

For cutting and shaping, use the following, shown in Fig. 1.8:
• Tenon saw, for cutting strip wood to length and making simple joints
• Hand saw, for long straight cuts. Hold at a low angle on plywood
• Hand-held electric jigsaw, for cutting out windows and doors, curved cuts and for joining up straight cuts (making the latter using a batten as a guide)
• Plane, for correcting thickness, chamfering and smoothing
• Wooden mallet and chisels – a narrow one 4–6 mm (³⁄₁₆–¼ in) for making grooves in battens for the plywood, and a broader one 18–25 mm (¾–1 in) for general shaping
• Hand drill
• Pliers
• Bench hook
For assembly, you only need those tools shown in Fig. 1.9:
• Screwdrivers, slot and crosshead types
• Hammer, small warrington type, for putting in panel pins. A heavy mallet is also useful for placing behind material to be pinned together

- Electric drill, which will drive hole saws.
- Hand-held circular saw, for long straight cuts. Ply sheets are unwieldy, so lay them on a piece of sawn 76 × 51 mm (3 × 2 in) timber, close to the intended cut. This will allow the blade to clear the ground or floor.
- Belt sander or orbital sander – this speeds things up. The belt sander trues up edges as it smoothes them.
- Plough plane – this hand tool is excellent for grooving window frames to fit the panels.

PAINTING THE PROJECTS

A wide range of shades and colours can be mixed up by your DIY shop, but a single project will not take even the smallest size tin of each colour you choose. The primary colours – red, blue and yellow – plus white and black give you the basis for the whole range of colours that you are likely to need for these projects. To darken a colour, add drops of black. To lighten, add small quantities of white. For very light colours, add small amounts of colour to a much larger quantity of white, as shown in Fig. 1.12. If you were to start with the colour, so much white would be needed that you would finish up with a wastefully large quantity.

Mixing the primaries yields secondaries, as shown in Fig. 1.13. You can vary the colour of each secondary by changing the proportions of the two primaries that make it. A spot of the third primary will reduce the brightness.

If you want to achieve a smooth finish, you need to remove all raised blemishes such as broken grain, whiskers and the like. Make sure that the points of panel pins are well clenched over and tapped down into the wood with a nail punch and hammer so that they are just below the surface. Fill hollows and open grain with decorator's cellulose-type filler, which is mixed with water. Do not make the mixture runny; that will raise the grain even more. Sand down so that only the hollows

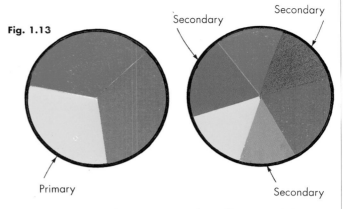

Fig. 1.13

Secondary
Secondary
Secondary
Primary
Secondary

are filled. Excess filler reduces the adhesion of the paint to the actual wood.

Fig 1.14 shows a much enlarged section of a finish in its various stages. The undercoat helps to level the surface still further, in addition to making a bond for the colour finishes. If you use emulsion paint, a few coats will bring the desired result, but for a gloss colour finish, the oil-based undercoats need to be sanded really smooth before the gloss goes on. Any bare wood showing will spoil the surface of the final coat.

Fig. 1.14

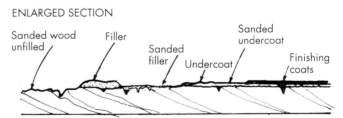

ENLARGED SECTION

Sanded wood unfilled
Filler
Sanded filler
Undercoat
Sanded undercoat
Finishing coats

Because the hinged corners of the walls have a slight gap for ease of action, daylight will show through. You can put a strip of weatherproof tape down the inside face, as in Fig. 1.15, then paint over it. The tape will fold with the walls when

Fig. 1.15

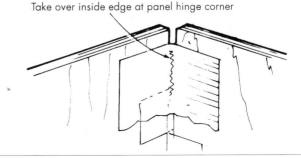

Take over inside edge at panel hinge corner

Fig. 1.12

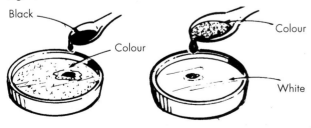

Black
Colour
Colour
White

they come inner face to inner face. However, on those joins that require the walls to fold the other way, you have to apply it to the outside, otherwise it will prevent the hinges working.

Fig 1.16 shows how to get a clean edge to a colour for decoration. Rub the masking tape down well along the edge where you will brush the second colour, and pull it back on itself as shown, just before the paint is touch dry.

Fig. 1.16

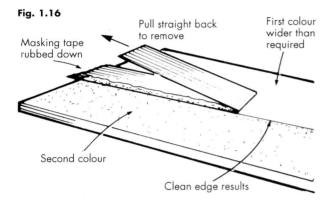

Masking tape rubbed down

Pull straight back to remove

First colour wider than required

Second colour

Clean edge results

Unless you have experience in hand-lettering with a brush, use the method shown in Fig 1.17. Thin pre-painted paper makes a good stick-on basis for cut-out letters or other artistic details. After you have glued them down with photo spray mount, apply clear varnish overall to seal the edges. If the rest of the paint job is matt finish, use matt varnish too. All finishes should be non-toxic types.

Fig. 1.17

Draw mirror letter on back of painted paper

Glue down on painted panel

Clear varnish over

SKILL RATING, COST AND CHILD HEIGHT

Each project has been awarded a star rating in terms of skill required, cost and child height. These ratings are relative – their main purpose is to allow comparisons to be made between the projects.

For skill, a * rating corresponds to the level of skill needed to put up a shelf; ***** would correspond to being able to make a coffee table.

The cost of each project depends principally on the amount of plywood required. For an average project with a two- or three-star rating, the cost would be approximately £35–£40.

The height ratings are only approximate – there is sufficient head-room for nearly all children within the anticipated age-range for which the projects are intended – up to age eight or nine.

SAFETY

Do not make structural changes or alter sizes of openings.

Always check that you have selected a suitable project to suit the intended recipient – be sure that heads or hands cannot get wedged in holes.

Pay particular attention to smoothing edges and corners. Leave no sharp points, and hold any loose locking pins in place with sticky tape.

* * * *

The author and publisher cannot be responsible for injury due to inappropriate selection of any project or improper workmanship.

Projects

Stable

A pony is often a firm favourite with children, even if it is not the real thing with all its necessary grazing, stable charges and fodder. In play terms a little stable, however simple, can really come to life when it has a working, wooden, puppet pony head, and a cloak. A young friend can then act with it, using it like a morris dance hobby-horse.

The stable is a 1016 mm (40 in)-square play-house, with working stable doors and a little window at the front. The roof slopes from a high scalloped fascia at the front, where 1345 mm (53 in) gives plenty of head-room for entry, to 1092 mm (43 in) at the back for stooping while grooming the pony and general cleaning up. There is another small window, and a place for fodder next to a dividing screen for the stall.

When you have painted the stable inside and out and added some real straw (or cut raffia) for the floor, hung up coils of rope and leather straps, and provided a seaside bucket and spade for 'mucking out', you have everything except the expenses and aroma. It folds up to a package only 152 mm (6 in) thick. Fig. 2.1 shows this easy project.

STAR RATING
Skill rating *
Cost **
Child height ****

1 Refer to Fig. 2.2 and, using the tape measure and pencil, mark out all the panel shapes, including the cut-out areas of windows.

If space is limited, tackle one sheet at a time. You can do the sawing work on top of the other sheets on the floor. There will be less stress on the sheet you are cutting if you move a spacing piece around underneath, kneeling over that while you work the portable saw or jigsaw.

Provided the space under the sheet you are cutting is greater than the sweep of the circular saw guard or the jigsaw blade stroke, then both tools and the ply underneath are safe. If you try to cut from the whole sheet while it stands upright, or if you cart it about from floor to bench and back, there is a chance that it may break at a narrow part. As soon as all the parts are cut from one sheet, lay them flat, without overlap, under the next sheet to be sawn – that is, unless there is somewhere close by, where they can be stacked level.

You will notice from the diagrams that many components share common saw cuts. The dimensions are for the centre of the saw 'kerf', or cut. The sizes of the finished play-house are not actually reduced by very much, because the hinges and joints make up the overall sizes and, in order to swing properly, doors need the clearance given by the saw cut.

Save offcuts for use later when you have to make smaller components and accessories. Keep those long narrow pieces flat while they await the saw.

MATERIALS

4 mm (³⁄₁₆ in) plywood: 3 sheets 2438 × 1219 mm (8 × 4 ft)
18 × 144 mm (¾ × 1¾ in) pine: 1 m (1 yd)
12 × 70 mm (½ × 2¾ in) pine: 406 mm (16 in)
18 × 18 mm (¾ in) pine: 1981 mm (78 in)
12 × 18 mm (½ × ¾ in) pine: 9 at 2 m (2 yd)
12 × 12 mm (½ in) pine: 2 at 2 m (2 yd)
9 mm (⅜ in) hardwood dowel: 203 mm (8 in)
6 mm (¼ in) hardwood dowel: 127 mm (5 in)

25 mm (1 in) strong upholstery webbing: 1 m (1 yd)
1 wire coat-hanger for cutting
20 mm (¾ in) panel pins
2 small staples
White rug wool: small quantity for mane
Fawn fabric for cloak: 1 m (1 yd)
Sewing thread
PVA glue
Glue sticks
Paint (to personal choice – non-toxic)

TOOLS

- Tenon saw
- Hand-held jigsaw
- Hand saw or hand-held circular saw
- Drill
- Chisels
- Plane
- Hammers
- Pliers
- G-cramps
- Sanding block and abrasive paper
- Pencil
- Try square
- Protractor
- Steel rule
- Steel tape
- Scissors
- Paint brushes

Fig. 2.1

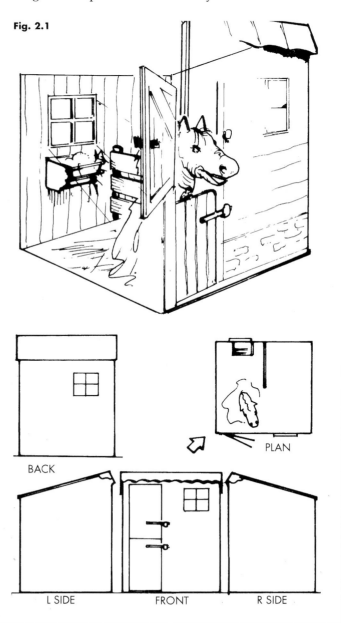

BACK

PLAN

L SIDE   FRONT   R SIDE

STABLE

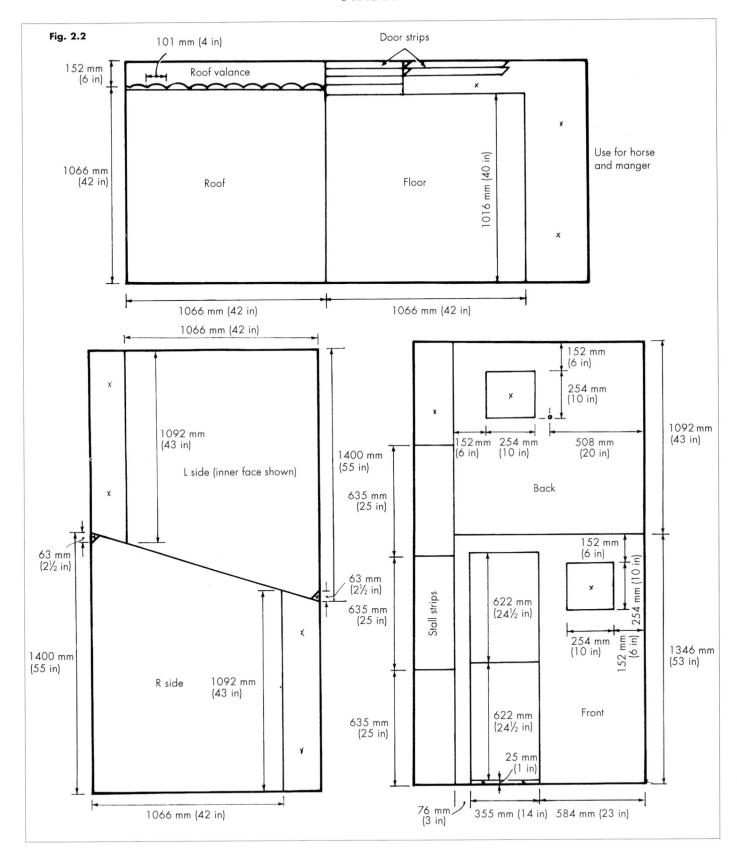

Fig. 2.2

101 mm (4 in)

Roof valance

Door strips

152 mm (6 in)

1066 mm (42 in)

Roof

Floor

1016 mm (40 in)

Use for horse and manger

1066 mm (42 in)

1066 mm (42 in)

1066 mm (42 in)

1092 mm (43 in)

L side (inner face shown)

1400 mm (55 in)

635 mm (25 in)

63 mm (2½ in)

63 mm (2½ in)

635 mm (25 in)

1400 mm (55 in)

R side

1092 mm (43 in)

635 mm (25 in)

1066 mm (42 in)

152 mm (6 in)

254 mm (10 in)

Back

152 mm (6 in)

254 mm (10 in)

508 mm (20 in)

1092 mm (43 in)

Stall strips

622 mm (24½ in)

152 mm (6 in)

254 mm (10 in)

254 mm (10 in)

152 mm (6 in)

1346 mm (53 in)

622 mm (24½ in)

Front

25 mm (1 in)

76 mm (3 in)

355 mm (14 in)

584 mm (23 in)

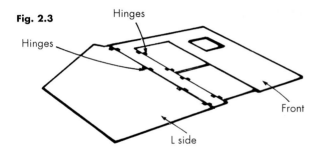

Fig. 2.3

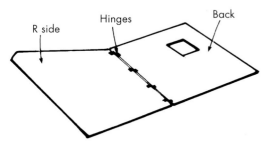

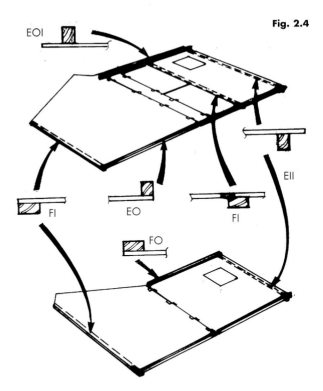

Fig. 2.4

2 When you have cut all the main plywood components, study Fig. 2.3, which shows which pieces are hinged together. Lay them out in the same order, one pair at a time, on a smooth, level and dust-free surface. A sheet of hardboard or plywood is ideal. Switch on the glue gun and, while it heats up, use scissors to cut the webbing into twenty-four 38 mm (1½ in) lengths.

3 Position the webbing strips in pairs, evenly spaced as shown, near the hinge lines, and glue them in place as described in the sequence shown in Chapter 1.

4 You now have two rather flexible pairs of walls. Using Fig. 2.4 as a reference, cut strips of 12 × 18 mm (½ × ¾ in) timber, which you should glue and fix with panel pins where indicated. It is best to measure from the actual panels. Use the tenon saw on this thin material, and mark their position with a pencil. To avoid misplacing them, use the letter reference shown on the drawing for both the panel and strips. Draw a line on the outer face for guidance when nailing inner strips, and on the inner face for those outside. The positions of the end strips should ensure that both pairs of walls align for assembly – i.e. a flat strip on one wall fits next to an inset edge-fixed strip on the next pair, as described in Chapter 1.

5 Lay a piece of 76 × 51 mm (3 × 2 in) timber for packing and support on the floor under the strip, and lay the panel over it. Check its position. Lift the panel and apply PVA glue to the strip. Lower the panel onto it and put a panel pin in each end to hold it. If it is positioned correctly, put in panel pins every 150 mm (about every 6 in). The pins will go right through the flat glued strips. This gives you the opportunity of making the joint stronger by clenching the points over when you have lifted the assembly from the packing wood. You should ease up the assembly with a screwdriver between packing and strip, otherwise the joint may open.

To clench the panel pins, knock the points sideways then force them back over into the wood, using a nail punch. You will need to have the job supported on the packing wood for this.

6 Measure enough 12 × 12 mm (½ in) wood to form the outer edges of the two window-frames. Form a shallow 1.5 mm (¹⁄₁₆ in) deep groove to take the plywood. Use a plough plane or a Stanley knife and narrow chisel to do this. Alternatively, if you have a small saw bench, a

Fig. 2.5

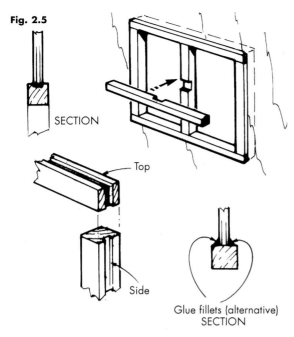

SECTION

Top

Side

Glue fillets (alternative)
SECTION

couple of light passes will do the same job.

Glue the head and sill strips in first, then the sides (stiles), which will hold them in place. Carefully cut the vertical bar to length, and form a halving joint with tenon saw and chisel to match a horizontal bar. Glue this and the ends into place, all as shown in Fig. 2.5.

You can opt for a less strong but quicker job by making the frame a tight fit without grooving it, gluing it in and running a bead of glue around both sides. However, the edges of the hole must be really true, whereas a tiny deviation would be hidden in the groove.

7 Stable doors are generally reinforced inside with a diagonal brace and rails top and bottom. Cut 38 mm (1½ in)-wide strips of ply or hard-

Fig. 2.6

Strips glued to inside face

Space to clear stop strip

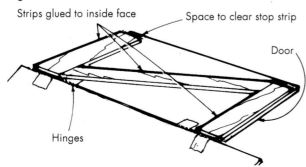

Door

Hinges

board and glue them to the inside of each door. (See Fig. 2.6.) Leave them short of the latch edge to clear the door stop strip which you fixed earlier, and with the door supported flat, put some weights on the strips while the glue sets.

8 Meanwhile make two latches from 18 mm (¾ in)-wide ply strips or pieces of 12 × 18 mm (½ × ¾ in) pine – see Fig. 2.7. The sockets for the latches on the door frame are outside and have a spacer thicker than the latches themselves (this is to prevent them sticking).

When the bracing is set on the doors, drill for 6 mm (¼ in) dowels which should pass loosely through the doors and tightly into the latches and shorter handles inside. This completes the major work on the walls.

Fig. 2.7

Drill to clear dowel through door

Handle, glue to dowel

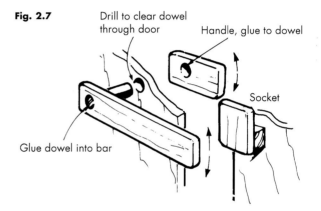

Socket

Glue dowel into bar

9 Open out the two pairs of walls to 90 degrees each, and bring the joint battens together. Drill 9 mm (⅜ in) holes 76 mm (3 in) from the top and bottom edges, to take dowels as in Fig. 2.8. Glue the dowels into the inset strips (EII type), and open the outer holes to easily clear the dowels. Drill a small hole across the protruding end of each dowel. This is to take a locking pin, which you bend from coat-hanger wire.

You can also apply this joint system to lock the walls to the floor panel, as shown in the lower part of the illustration.

10 One panel of plywood forms the roof. Edge this with 12 × 18 mm (½ × ¾ in) strip glued on edge underneath. Using the jigsaw, cut the wavy-edged fascia from an offcut of plywood and when the front edge strip has set hard, glue and

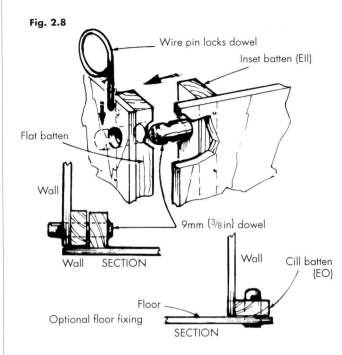

Fig. 2.8

Wire pin locks dowel

Inset batten (EII)

Flat batten

Wall

Wall SECTION

9mm (³⁄₈in) dowel

Wall

Cill batten (EO)

Floor

Optional floor fixing

SECTION

pin the fascia to it. The joint will be a right angle so that the fascia tilts when the roof is on the walls. At this stage, check it for fit and saw off any of the top edge that interferes with the seating at the front corners.

11 Now mark out and saw a pair of brackets from the 12 × 70 mm (½ × 2¾ in) offcut. Glue and pin these as shown in Fig. 2.9. It is best to fix them to the side strips before pinning through the fascia. If you do it the other way round, it will slide back.

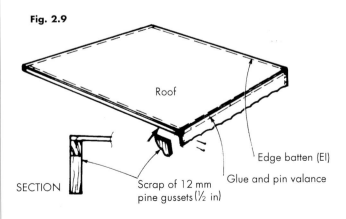

Fig. 2.9

Roof

SECTION

Scrap of 12 mm pine gussets (½ in)

Edge batten (EI)

Glue and pin valance

12 The dividing partition is slatted. Make it from three pieces of plywood offcut about 200 mm (8 in) wide – the exact width is not important. Leave 25 mm (1 in) gaps between each strip, and at the bottom. Glue and pin the strips to the 18 × 18 mm (¾ in) upright and an offcut of 12 × 18 mm (½ × ¾ in) pine, which goes next to the back wall as in Fig. 2.10.

Cut out the floor panel if you have not already done so, set up the walls upon it and mark the position of the front and rear uprights on its centre line. Glue short pieces of 12 × 18 mm (½ × ¾ in) pine to the floor to form locating sockets, as shown in the same drawing.

With the roof off, lean the partition against one side wall and slide it back to meet the back wall panel (not a corner strip). Mark its position on the side wall, then mark the height of the wall on the front upright, and cut it to this angle. Drill into the cut end and glue in a piece of 9 mm (³⁄₈ in) dowel. Measure the distance of the mark on the side wall and transfer it to the roof centre line. Drill this for the dowel, which will pass through when the roof is on.

13 Using strong pliers, bend an upward-facing hook from coat-hanger wire as shown in Fig. 2.10 and force it into holes in the partition, then reinforce it with webbing and hot-melt glue. Drill the back wall for it, and insert the hook while the partition is tilted back. When back in its sockets, the hook should lock in the hole.

Fig. 2.10

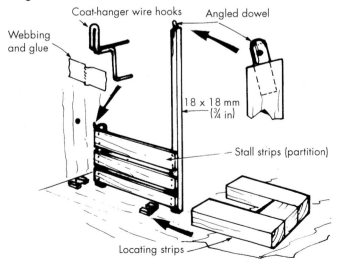

Coat-hanger wire hooks

Angled dowel

Webbing and glue

18 × 18 mm (¾ in)

Stall strips (partition)

Locating strips

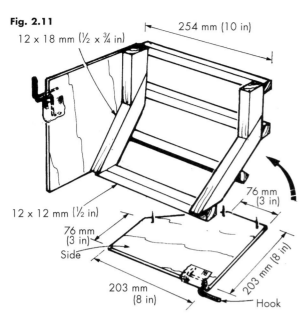

Fig. 2.11

12 × 18 mm (½ × ¾ in)

254 mm (10 in)

12 × 12 mm (½ in)

76 mm (3 in)

76 mm (3 in)

Side

203 mm (8 in)

203 mm (8 in)

Hook

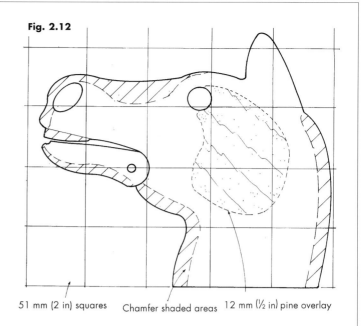

Fig. 2.12

51 mm (2 in) squares — Chamfer shaded areas — 12 mm (½ in) pine overlay

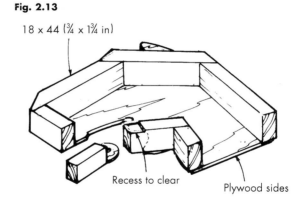

Fig. 2.13

18 × 44 (¾ × 1¾ in)

Recess to clear — Plywood sides

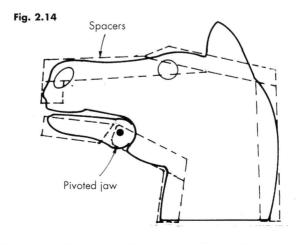

Fig. 2.14

Spacers

Pivoted jaw

14 Fig 2.11 shows how to construct the manger, which goes under the back window. Use more plywood offcuts and short pieces of strip to provide a seating for the four cross-strips of 12 × 12 mm (½ in) pine. Cut and glue up the side assemblies together as a pair for left and right positions. Mark the positions of the cross-strips while they are clamped together. When dry, support each end in turn in a vice and glue and pin each rail in place. Finally make two more wire hooks and fix them as you did on the partition. Sand off the sharp edges of the rails.

15 The pony starts as a flat-sided box. Draw out the shape of the outline on plywood off-cuts, using the gridded drawing in Fig. 2.12. Pin two pieces of plywood together and saw as one with the jigsaw. Now mark the shaded areas, to serve as a guide when you start to shape the head. While you have the drawing handy, mark out, by drawing the grid on a couple of offcuts of 12 mm (½ in) board that remains. These are the doublers which represent the cheeks.

16 Cut pieces of 18 × 44 mm (¾ × 1¾ in) pine to space the plywood outlines apart. Chamfer the ends at their joints, as shown in Fig. 2.13, and recess the lower one to allow the jaw to swivel freely. The spacer strips do not lie flush, but protrude slightly, as in Fig. 2.14. Check that both ply sides give the same amount of spacer showing when you glue them in place. Leave them clamped up until dry, then glue on the cheek doublers. At this stage the jaw is free on a loose dowel, which you now pull out. Put in two staples as shown in Fig. 2.15 and tie a piece of string to the jaw, before replacing the dowel. Now the jaw will snap shut when the string is pulled.

Fig. 2.15

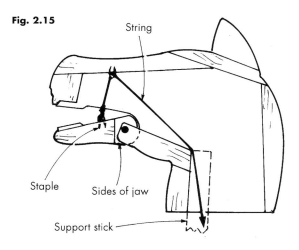

17 Clamp the head in a vice with a scrap of 44 mm (1¾ in)-thick packing inserted in the neck. Using the wide chisel and wooden mallet, carve away the edge of the plywood and part of the spacers, to form rounded edges, up to the guide lines that you drew earlier. Shave the edges of the cheeks right down to blend into the flat plywood sides.

18 Now drill out the eye sockets and nostrils and form a slight groove to the rear of the latter as shown in Fig. 2.16. Recess the plywood to form upper teeth, and then insert into the eye sockets two halves of a plastic ball taken from a roll-on deodorant. When you have blended these into the cheek piece and generally filled unwanted hollows with car body filler, it should look more realistic. The eye detail may be useful when you paint the head. The prototype head is light brown and is set off with a white mane which you can make from strands of rug wool sewen together. Saw a slit in the neck and top of the head for the mane, and glue it in. Glue and screw a stick into the front of the neck for use as a hobby horse, or ask the needlework member of the household to

make a cloak to be gathered and stapled around the neck after the style of a morris dancer's hobby-horse.

19 Sand off any rough or sharp edges and corners on the play-house, and smooth grain which may have escaped earlier notice. Fill hollows flush with decorator's filler and smooth off when dry. Sand lightly and paint. If the play-house is to be used indoors and outdoors only in good weather, you can use emulsion paint. It looks well with light-coloured upper walls and dark lower half, representing old brickwork. Rule horizontal lines in a slightly deeper shade of the upper part to represent clapboard. Paint the doors and window-frames a deep dull red and repeat this on the fascia. The roof itself can be dark grey or dark green. You need the maximum light inside, so paint all white here, with a dirty buff floor.

Fig. 2.16

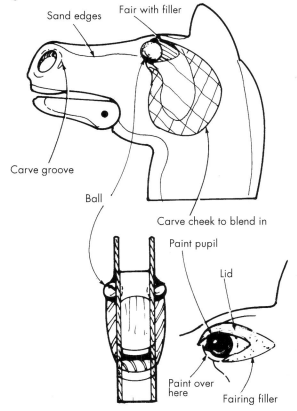

Hospital

Hospitals are another popular play theme, where the patient is often a long-suffering younger sister or brother, or a favourite teddy. Open the door of the compact 1016 mm (40 in)-square play-house, shown in Fig. 3.1: on the right, under a roof light, there is an operating theatre, with table and instrument trolley. Near the front there is a place for dispensing prescriptions, which can be handed through a window hatch to out-patients.

Swing a curtain across to screen off the theatre part, and there, on the left, another window lights the ward. This contains one bed for a tiny tot, or toy, and its own locker and visitor's stool. The curtain both draws on its rail, and swivels round to either side, so the area near the door becomes a waiting room. The maximum headroom is 1219 mm (48 in) and the door is 1041 mm (41 in) high.

All the fittings and accessories form part of the project. There are no complicated joints and the basic play-house folds to a package only 152 mm (6 in) thick, leaving the furniture to be used as separate playthings.

STAR RATING
Skill rating **
Cost **
Child height ****

MATERIALS

4 mm (3/16 in) plywood:
  3 sheets 2438 × 1219 mm (8 × 4 ft)
18 × 51 mm (3/4 × 2 in) pine: 660 mm (26 in)
18 × 18 mm (3/4 in) pine:
  4 at 304 mm (12 in)
  8 at 457 mm (18 in)
12 × 18 mm (1/2 × 3/4 in) pine: 6 at 1092 mm (43 in)
  2 at 1066 mm (42 in)
  9 at 1016 mm (40 in)
12 × 12 mm (1/2 in) pine:
  2 at 559 mm (22 in)
  4 at 533 mm (21 in)
  2 at 381 mm (15 in)
  3 at 330 mm (13 in)
  4 at 266 mm (10½ in)
  2 at 177 mm (7 in)

9 mm (3/8 in) hardwood dowel: 1 m (1 yd)
2 mm (3/32 in) clear styrene glazing: 254 × 254 mm (10 in)
4 25 mm (1 in) no. 10 roundhead woodscrews
Light curtain fabric: 1.25 m (1¼ yd)
10 curtain rings
Curtain wire
Coat-hanger wire
25 mm (1 in)-wide strong upholstery webbing: 1.5 m (1½ yd)
PVA glue
Glue sticks
20 mm (3/4 in) panel pins
Sewing thread
Filler
Non-toxic paint

TOOLS
- Hand saw, or hand-held circular saw
- Tenon saw
- Hand-held jigsaw
- Plane
- Chisels
- Drill
- Screwdriver
- Hammer
- Nail punch
- Strong pliers
- Scissors
- Glue gun
- Domestic iron
- Abrasive paper
- Pencil
- Rule
- Try square
- G-cramps
- Filling knife
- Paint brushes

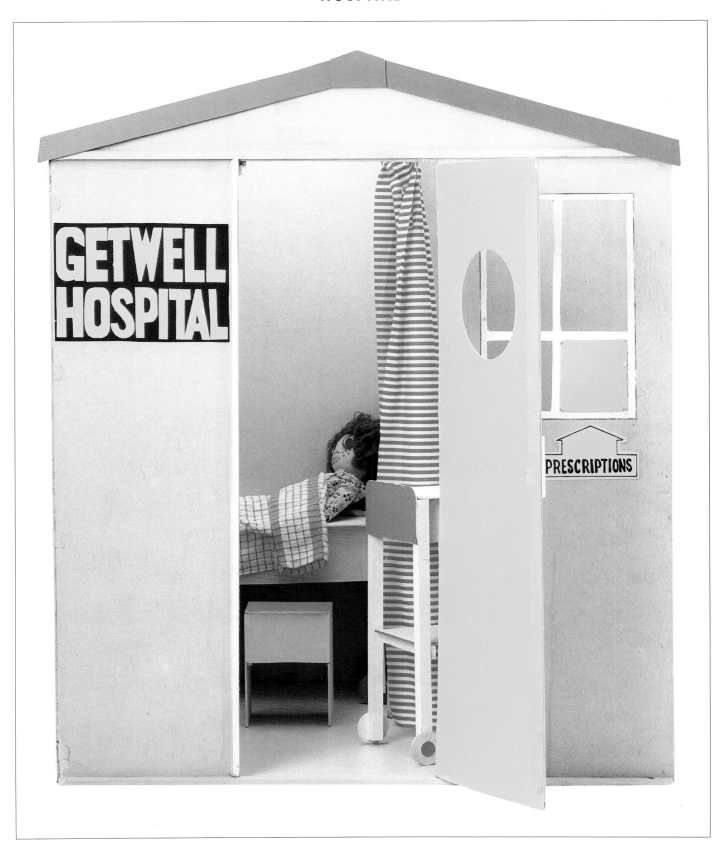

1 Tackle the three sheets of plywood separately; begin by marking out the basic panel shapes, as shown opposite in Fig. 3.2. (Measure carefully: some panels share the same saw cut, so an error on one will also affect the adjacent piece.) The slight reduction in panel size caused by the saw cut (kerf) will give the necessary clearance for doors and panel joint hinges. Saw down the line where panels are adjacent and on the waste side for other cuts. As you separate the panels, keep all the parts flat – otherwise, if you leave them overnight, they may warp. All the projects gain their full strength when complete, and maintain their shape when assembled, or when correctly stored against a flat surface.

2 Smooth the the sawn edge of the panels where the hinges are to go – Fig. 3.3. Switch on the glue gun and, with scissors, cut 35 pieces of webbing, each 38 mm (1½ in) long. Lay them in pairs as shown, except for three on the tiny window hatch (formed from the waste of the window pane).

Position the panels and door as shown and spot-fix each tape on alternate sides, as described in Chapter 1. Smooth them flat with the domestic iron, which will saturate the webbing and bond it fully. Turn the whole set of of pieces over and finish off in the same way. You now should have two pairs of walls, the door and hatch and the pitched roof all hinged in sets. Keep them flat.

Fig. 3.1

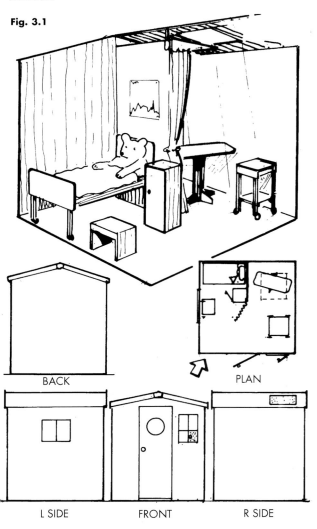

BACK

PLAN

L SIDE   FRONT   R SIDE

Fig. 3.3

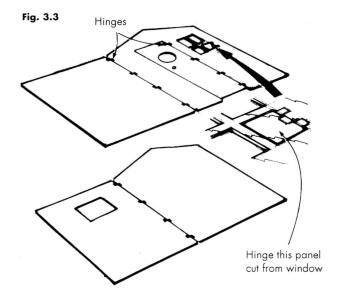

Hinges

Hinge this panel cut from window

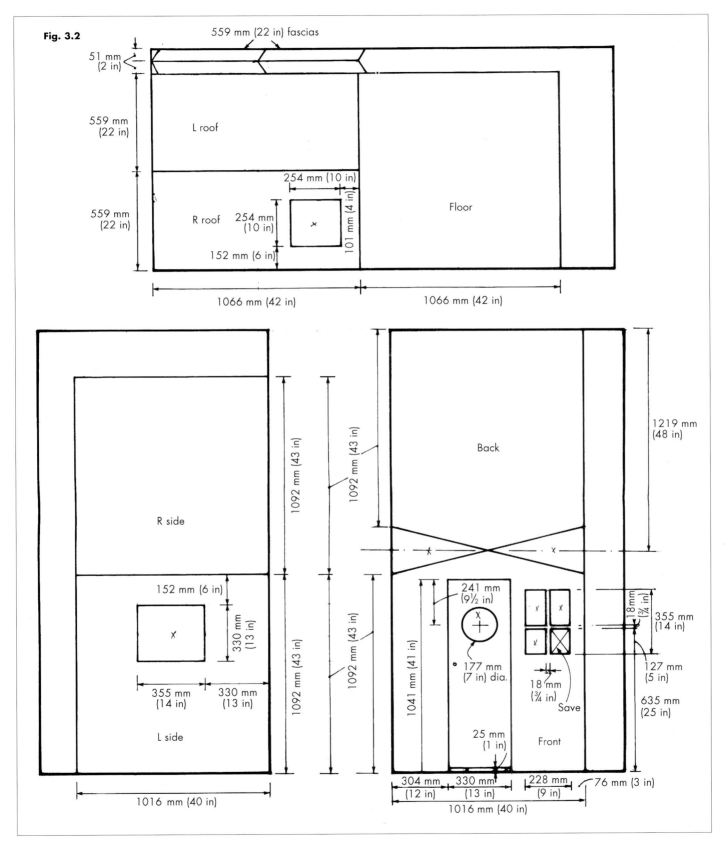

Fig. 3.2

559 mm (22 in) fascias

51 mm (2 in)

559 mm (22 in) — L roof

559 mm (22 in) — R roof

254 mm (10 in)

254 mm (10 in)

101 mm (4 in)

152 mm (6 in)

Floor

1066 mm (42 in)

1066 mm (42 in)

R side

152 mm (6 in)

330 mm (13 in)

355 mm (14 in)

330 mm (13 in)

L side

1016 mm (40 in)

1092 mm (43 in)

1092 mm (43 in)

1092 mm (43 in)

1092 mm (43 in)

1092 mm (43 in)

Back

1219 mm (48 in)

241 mm (9½ in)

177 mm (7 in) dia.

18 mm (¾ in)

355 mm (14 in)

127 mm (5 in)

18 mm (¾ in)

Save

1041 mm (41 in)

635 mm (25 in)

25 mm (1 in)

Front

304 mm (12 in)

330 mm (13 in)

228 mm (9 in)

76 mm (3 in)

1016 mm (40 in)

Fig. 3.4

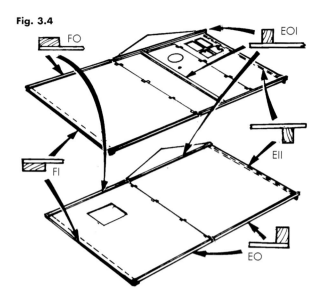

Fig. 3.6

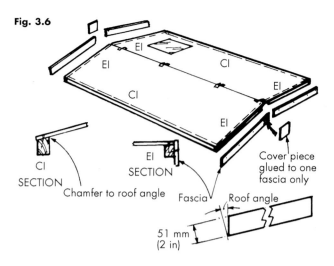

Cover piece glued to one fascia only

Chamfer to roof angle

Fascia   Roof angle

51 mm (2 in)

3 Using glue and panel pins, attach the 12 × 18 mm (½ × ¾ in) battens, as shown in Fig. 3.4. Notice which are on edge and which are laid flat, on inner and outer faces of the plywood. Be careful not to accidentally turn any pair of walls the wrong way up. This work is best done on the floor, using a length of 51 × 76 mm (2 × 3 in) timber as a support underneath. Move it around as required. The panel pins will go right through the flat battens; clench them over flush after each complete batten is in place. (Do not leave the clenching until later, or you will get scratched.)

4 Following Fig. 3.5, saw strips of 12 × 12 mm (½ in) pine to fit around, and under, the hole in the right-hand roof panel. They should overlap the edge by only 4 mm (³⁄₁₆ in). Butt join the corners, when you glue and pin.

Cut a panel of plastic (styrene) glazing, ready to drop into the rebate so formed. Do not fix it yet, to avoid scratching it.

Fig. 3.5

Styrene glazing after painting

Hinges

12 x 12 mm (½ in) frame

SECTION

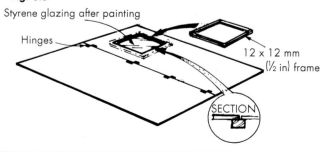

5 With a plane, chamfer the short edge of two strips of 12 × 18 mm (½ × ¾ in) pine, which form the eaves. Cut, glue and pin pieces of 12 × 12 mm (½ in) pine under the short ends, as in Fig. 3.6, then fix the chamfered strips in the same way. Clench the protruding pins. Now with the square strips supported against a heavy block of wood, glue and pin the narrow plywood gable facing. Clench these pins too.

6 The front window is best left with its fretted-out panes, so turn now to the side window. Form a shallow groove in the edge of the short pieces of 12 × 12 mm (½ in) pine, to fit over the edge of the plywood opening as in Fig. 3.7. Trim

Fig. 3.7

Groove for wall

Groove

Cut to fit

Groove ends of top and bottom

Groove sides

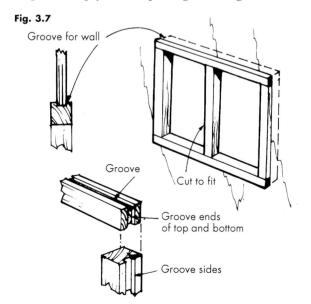

the strip to length as necessary; the ends of top and bottom strips need grooves too. With these in place, measure for the sides and centre strip. Make these a good fit, then glue them all in place.

7 The floor panel needs no battens; when you have cut it out, lay it down and position each pair of walls on its edges. When the walls are hinged out at right angles, the flat batten on one end of each pair should rest against the edge batten on the other pair. Hold them together with a G-cramp at the top, then using a 9 mm (⅜ in) bit, drill right through both strips 76 mm (3 in) from the top and bottom edges. Repeat on the other corner.

Separate the pairs of panels, and with a size larger drill open up the holes in the flat battens and walls to easily clear pieces of 9 mm (⅜ in) dowel. Glue the latter into the edge-glued strips, with a glue fillet for extra security. When dry, pass them through the now reassembled panels and mark the protruding end for drilling a small hole across to take a coat-hanger wire locking pin, as shown in Chapter 1.

8 Now start on the inside details. The partition between the ward and theatre has to be hinged so that it folds flat for storage. Make this up as shown in Fig. 3.8. Begin with more hinging. Drill the ends of the edge strip and fit pieces of dowel – short at the bottom, to enter a hole in the floor, and long at the top, to carry a curtain bracket, then enter a hole in the roof. Fix the narrow strip to the centre of the back wall.

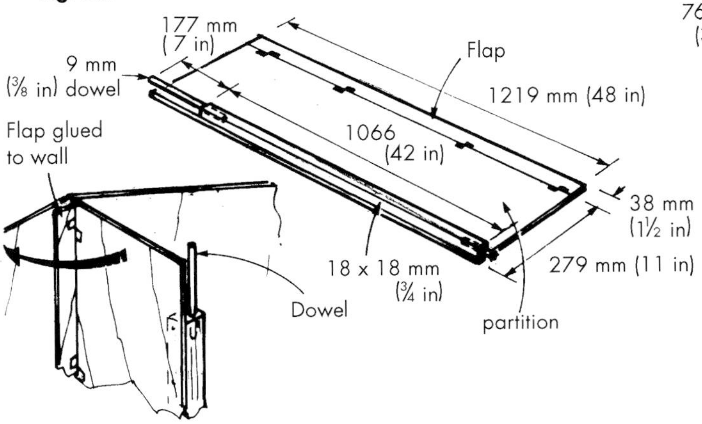

9 Cut a wire coat-hanger and, with pliers, bend it to form the curtain rail as shown in Fig. 3.9. Do not squeeze the small loop 'A' tight: you have to allow the curtain rings to slide onto the rail, and it is easier to sew them to the curtain before they do so. Make the loops large enough to ride easily on the dowel, so that you can swing the rail around like a gate.

Fig. 3.9

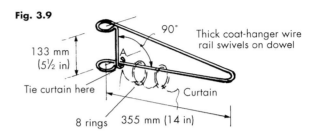

10 The bed is shown in Fig. 3.10. Start by making four dummy castors by cutting out disks 51 mm (2 in) dia. from a plywood offcut. With the tenon saw, make a slit to take a disk in the end of each leg, which is a 304 mm (12 in) piece of 18 × 18 mm (¾ in) strip. Do not glue the disks in yet, just check for fit.

From more plywood offcuts, with the outer grain running lengthwise, cut the main panel, head and foot panels and a pair of side strips all to the sizes shown in the drawing. Sand the edges smooth.

Fig. 3.8

Fig. 3.10

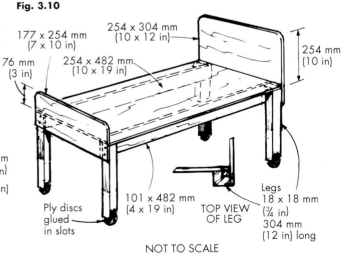

11 Glue and pin the side strips to the inside faces of the legs. Using a try square, check that they are at right angles and flush with the top edge and the ends. When dry, rest each leg on the edge of the workbench, or clamp it in the vice to support it while you glue and pin the head, then the foot, to the legs. You may find that a G-cramp on the previous joint also steadies the job while you do this.

12 Stand the bed on its feet. It may still be flexible. No matter; if you have cut the main panel to the correct length it should stiffen the bed. Apply glue to the top of each rail, the top of each of the legs, and one end of the main panel. Drop this in place and pin it to the top of each leg.

Turn the bed over and run beads of glue along the foot joint and along the inner faces of the rails. Leave it upside down until the glue has gone past the runny stage, then glue and insert a disk into each leg slot. Now turn it right way up and rest it on a level surface to harden.

13 Now for the locker; cut more panels from the offcuts of plywood, outer grain on the longest dimension. The sizes are shown in Fig. 3.11. Out with the hinging tackle again, and decide which way you want the door to swing.

With the door hinged to one side panel, glue and pin battens to the inner faces of the sides, left- and right-handed. Measure and mark for identical positions of the shelf rails, which you fix last. Clench the protruding points of the pins.

14 When the glue has set, glue and pin the locker top and bottom in position, then turn it on its face and glue and pin the back to the 12 × 12 mm (½ in) side battens. Pin through into the top and bottom cross rails, with two intermediate pins in each corner strip. They will be easier to clench than if they were near the corners. Glue the shelf in afterwards, or leave it loose. Fit a small screw-on knob and a small patch of Velcro to act as a catch. Do not fix the locker to the folding partition.

15 The operating table is shown in Fig. 3.12. Start by shaping the top and foot rails from 18 × 51 mm (¾ × 2 in) pine (the exact thickness is not important).

Cut the plywood foot to fit over the foot rail; while you have the saw handy, cut out the top panel, rounding off the corners. Mark the centre of the top and foot rails on each side, allowing for the thickness of the ply foot, which you now glue to the foot rail. Glue and pin two of the 457 mm

Fig. 3.11

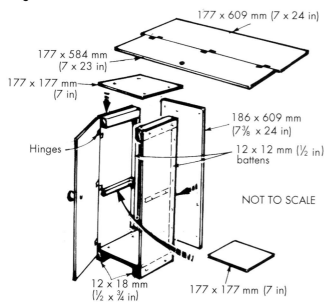

177 x 609 mm (7 x 24 in)
177 x 584 mm (7 x 23 in)
177 x 177 mm (7 in)
Hinges
186 x 609 mm (7⅜ x 24 in)
12 x 12 mm (½ in) battens
NOT TO SCALE
12 x 18 mm (½ x ¾ in)
177 x 177 mm (7 in)

Fig. 3.12

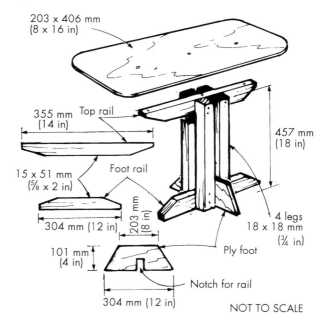

203 x 406 mm (8 x 16 in)
355 mm (14 in) Top rail
457 mm (18 in)
15 x 51 mm (⅝ x 2 in)
Foot rail
304 mm (12 in)
203 mm (8 in)
4 legs 18 x 18 mm (¾ in)
Ply foot
101 mm (4 in)
Notch for rail
304 mm (12 in)
NOT TO SCALE

(18 in)-long pieces of 18 × 18 mm (¾ in) pine, one each side of the foot rail (apply glue to the notch in the ply foot and to each side).

Turn the job over and glue and pin the other pair of legs in position in the same way. Finally, glue and pin the top onto the top rail and tops of all four legs.

You now have a cantilever-style operating table.

16 The trolley shown in Fig. 3.13 can be used to carry instruments, 'medicines', or toy patients. Construct the top in the same manner as the bed. It uses the remaining four strips of 18 × 18 mm (¾ in) for the legs. Following the dimensions shown, glue and pin a couple of 12 × 18 mm (½ × ¾ in) strips across the legs to support the bottom shelf, which improves rigidity.

Unlike those on the bed, the trolley's wheels (castors) are functional. Cut 76 mm (3 in) diameter disks of ply with the jigsaw, or if you have one, a hole-saw on an electric drill. In the latter case choose a woodscrew that fits the 6 mm (¼ in) centre hole of each. You will need a metal washer to space each wheel from its leg, otherwise it will bind. If you drill the hole for each screw in a slightly upward direction, each wheel will lean away from the leg, and its contact with the floor will be nearer to the load. This too, will reduce the chance of binding.

Fig. 3.13

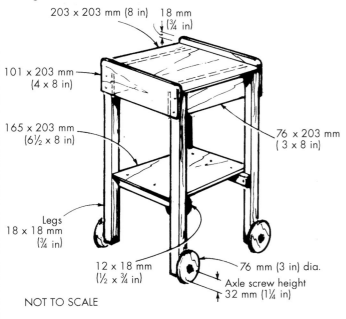

203 x 203 mm (8 in)   18 mm (¾ in)

101 x 203 mm (4 x 8 in)

165 x 203 mm (6½ x 8 in)

76 x 203 mm (3 x 8 in)

Legs 18 x 18 mm (¾ in)

12 x 18 mm (½ x ¾ in)

76 mm (3 in) dia.

Axle screw height 32 mm (1¼ in)

NOT TO SCALE

You may choose to use small furniture castors instead – these should be of the plug-in type, but reinforce the bottom of each leg with a couple of turns of webbing applied with PVA glue. After making the trolley, go over it to check all the joints, reinforcing with beads of glue where necessary. Trolleys come in for some rough treatment!

17 The visitor's stool is box-like and is shown in Fig. 3.14. Cut the panels to the size shown from the remainder of the plywood offcuts and reinforce the joints with short pieces of 12 × 18 mm (½ × ¾ in) pine which you glue and pin to the sides, which are set back to accommodate the plywood cross rails. Clench the panel pin points over, before gluing and pinning the top and the cross rails in place. You may wish to use small woodscrews for this last stage, but pilot drill carefully so that they do not break out of the inner edges of the strips.

Fig. 3.14

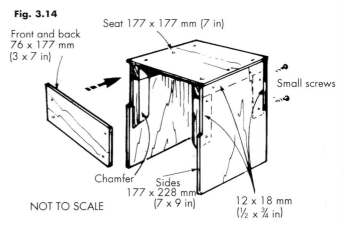

Seat 177 x 177 mm (7 in)

Front and back 76 x 177 mm (3 x 7 in)

Small screws

Chamfer   Sides 177 x 228 mm (7 x 9 in)

12 x 18 mm (½ x ¾ in)

NOT TO SCALE

18 Now comes the task of carefully smoothing all of the hospital's sharp corners and exposed edges, using a sanding block and progressively finer grades of abrasive paper. A belt sander will do the job very quickly, but the construction is lightweight and if you remove too much material the shape may suffer. In any case, keep any sanding away from the hinges; these will fray if abraded. Rough spots here can be smoothed with the hot domestic iron. Rather than trying to hide them, let the hinges express themselves as part of the structure.

Have a final check that all the clenched pins are flush and that in the clenching process, the heads have not been made to protrude on the other faces. If so, hold a heavy mallet on the opposite side while you drive them flush.

With a filling knife, wipe some decorator's filler along such battens to conceal the pins and level the surface again. Fill any gaps at joints and surface hollows; when dry, sand before painting.

Use light colours inside the hospital and white for the operating theatre and its furniture. The ward part can be light pink to make the 'patient' look better. There will be some curtain material left over from the swinging screen. Cut in half, this can go each side of the ward window on curtain spring. Drill holes in the wall and use opened-out hooks to fit them.

The colour of the outside is your choice, but have the door and window frames, and the gable end of the roof, a strong colour. Fix the styrene glazing in the roof light with dabs of hot-melt glue, but only after painting the roof inside and out. There is no glazing in the other windows, so as to allow necessary ventilation for the users.

Boutique

What little girl does not like to dress up? Why not, then, make her the owner of a dress shop? This one has a glazed display window, a little counter, changing cubicle and clothes rail, plus clothes-hanger heads, for the window, and a floor-standing dummy.

All fit into a 1016 mm (40 in)-square play-house with a similar roof to the hospital project. The shop window has a box frame to make it protrude, and the roof is hidden behind a shop nameplate panel. The boutique folds down to under 152 mm (6 in) flat.

There is less work in the accessories than in the previous project, and the general appearance is contemporary, as you can see from the photograph and Fig. 4.1.

STAR RATING
Skill rating **
Cost **
Child height ****

MATERIALS

4 mm plywood: 3 sheets 2438 × 1219 mm (8 × 4 ft)

9 × 95 mm (⅜ × 3¾ in) pine cladding for cutting: 2 at 635 mm (25 in)
2 at 533 mm (21 in)

12 × 18 mm (½ × ¾ in) pine: 5 at 1143 mm (45 in)
2 at 1041 mm (41 in)
8 at 1016 mm (40 in)
3 at 762 mm (30 in)
2 at 508 mm (20 in)

12 × 12 mm (½ in) pine:
2 at 508 mm (20 in)
2 at 355 mm (14 in)
2 at 330 mm (13 in)
4 at 279 mm (11 in)

9 mm (⅜ in) hardwood dowel: 1 m (1 yd)

2 mm (³⁄₃₂ in) clear styrene glazing: 1 at 648 × 521 mm (25½ × 20½ in)
1 at 254 × 254 mm (10 in)

Styrene mirror: about 508 × 254 mm (20 × 10 in)

25 mm (1 in)-wide strong upholstery webbing: 2 m (2 yd)

Light curtain fabric: 1.5 m (1½ yd)

Curtain rings

Sewing thread

Small drawer handle

2 wooden spring-type clothes pegs

20 mm (¾ in) panel pins

Coat-hanger wire

PVA glue

Glue sticks

Decorator's filler

Non-toxic paint

TOOLS

- Hand saw, or hand-held circular saw
- Tenon saw
- Hand-held jigsaw
- Plane
- Chisels
- Drill
- Hammer
- Nail punch
- Glue gun
- Domestic iron
- Sander, or sanding block
- Abrasive paper
- Pencil
- Rule
- Try square
- G-cramps
- Filling knife
- Paint brushes

packing, which should also be thick enough to clear the saw guard as it swings round underneath.

2 Smooth the edges that are to be hinged – Fig. 4.3 shows which panels are to be linked. Remember to note which side is the outer one, otherwise one panel might finish up a mirror image of how it should be!

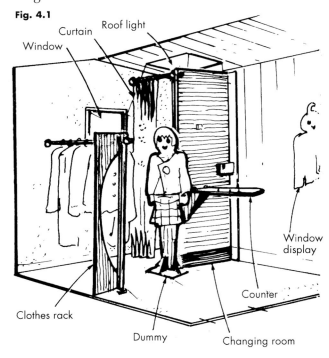

Fig. 4.1

Curtain / Roof light / Window / Window display / Counter / Changing room / Dummy / Clothes rack

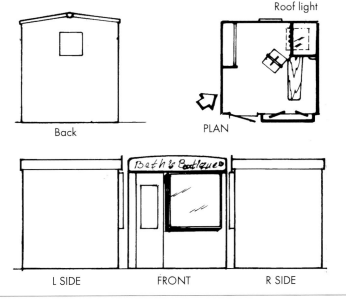

Back / Roof light / PLAN / L SIDE / FRONT / R SIDE / Beth's Boutique

1 Mark out, pencil on the name of each part, and saw each of the three plywood boards, according to Fig. 4.2. Do one at a time, keeping the cut pieces and the strips of waste flat until needed. You will need to make smaller items from this collection of offcuts, so it too should be warp-free.

You will need the jigsaw for cutting across the top of the door and removing the waste from the windows. When doing this, lay the panel on a spacing strip of thick timber, drill a hole for the jigsaw blade to enter and join up straight cuts for the door. You need two holes, one in each diagonal corner, to start the two pairs of cuts for the windows. Keep the spacing timber close to the cutting line, but avoid hitting it with the blade when you change direction. For long straight cuts, a hand-held circular saw is preferable to a hand saw. Use the same

BOUTIQUE

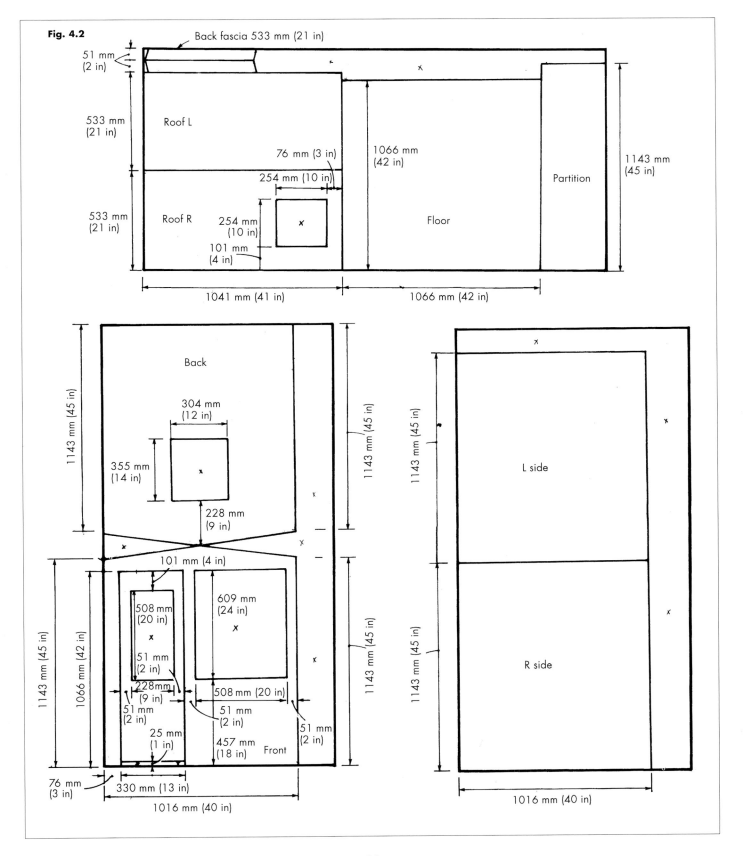

Fig. 4.2

Back fascia 533 mm (21 in)

51 mm (2 in)

533 mm (21 in) — Roof L

533 mm (21 in) — Roof R

76 mm (3 in)

254 mm (10 in)

254 mm (10 in)

101 mm (4 in)

1066 mm (42 in)

1143 mm (45 in)

Partition

Floor

1041 mm (41 in)

1066 mm (42 in)

Back

1143 mm (45 in)

304 mm (12 in)

355 mm (14 in)

228 mm (9 in)

1143 mm (45 in)

101 mm (4 in)

508 mm (20 in)

609 mm (24 in)

51 mm (2 in)

228 mm (9 in)

508 mm (20 in)

51 mm (2 in)

51 mm (2 in)

51 mm (2 in)

25 mm (1 in)

457 mm (18 in)

Front

1143 mm (45 in)

1066 mm (42 in)

1143 mm (45 in)

76 mm (3 in)

330 mm (13 in)

1016 mm (40 in)

L side

R side

1143 mm (45 in)

1143 mm (45 in)

1143 mm (45 in)

1016 mm (40 in)

Cut a supply of 38 mm (1½ in)-long strips of webbing with scissors and lay in pairs down the hinge lines. Using the glue gun, spot fix them alternately left and right along one edge, then with the domestic iron on the hottest setting, flatten the glued halves of each hinge. This will spread the reheated glue into the weave and strengthen it. Lift each panel, wipe the iron over the edge at each hinge to make it lean around the joint. Turn the panels over and fold each hinge out to be glued to its opposite panel in the same way. You can rectify mistakes by reironing to soften the glue.

3 The reinforcing strips, which you fix with PVA glue and panel pins, go on now. Study Fig. 4.4 and select which of the 12 × 18 mm (½ × ¾ in) strips are to go under the panels, which you should now position outer side up on the floor. The key

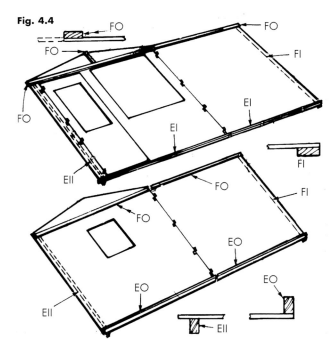

Fig. 4.4

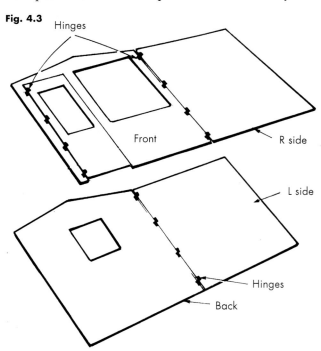

Fig. 4.3 Hinges

Front

R side

L side

Hinges

Back

sketches around them will show which strips are flat and which are on their edge. Take the packing strip that you used when sawing, and slide it under where each strip is to go. This will support the job evenly, and any panel pins which go through the flat strips can be clenched later, rather than buckling on a hard floor. Do all the inner strips on a pair of panels first, turn the job over, clench protruding points, and then do the outer ones.

4 The box frame of the shop window incorporates a rebate for the plastic glazing (glass is not recommended for play things). Take the thin pine cladding strip and carefully saw a 12 mm (½ in)-wide strip from the ready-grooved edge. Save this undamaged channel section until later – see Fig. 4.5.

Trim off the tongued edge from the cladding. This will leave a plain strip of wood to form the box. Glue and pin top and bottom strips to the side pieces, which are the same depth as the opening. Put the panel face down and glue and pin them from the back. Trim the ready-grooved pieces to fit on the front edges, but keep them on one side with the styrene panel which you cut to fit (these go on after painting).

Fig. 4.5

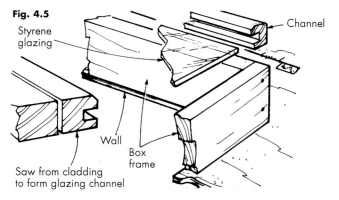

Styrene glazing

Channel

Wall

Box frame

Saw from cladding to form glazing channel

5 Glue and pin strips of 12 × 12 mm (½ in) pine to the front of the door around the window cut-out. The vertical strips are the size of the hole, the top and bottom butt against them as in Fig. 4.6.

Fig. 4.6

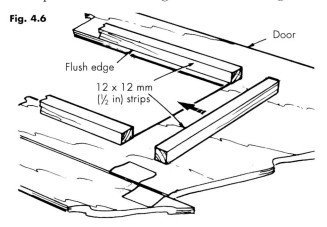

Door

Flush edge

12 x 12 mm (½ in) strips

6 Use more of the same strip to line the back window. Make a shallow groove in the outer edge with a tenon saw or chisel, to fit over the edge of the plywood. It need only be 1.5 mm (¹⁄₁₆ in) deep – see Fig. 4.7. Push the top and bottom strips into place and hold them there with the side pieces. Use PVA glue all round and at the corners.

Fig. 4.7

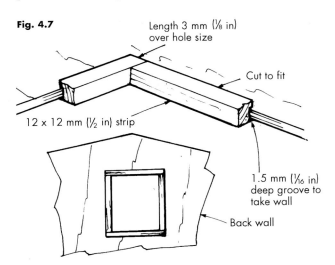

Length 3 mm (⅛ in) over hole size

Cut to fit

12 x 12 mm (½ in) strip

1.5 mm (¹⁄₁₆ in) deep groove to take wall

Back wall

7 Shape a piece of long ply offcut to a pleasing curve, to sit over door and shop window. Round off the edges and glue and pin it to the flat strip on the front wall panel. Fig. 4.8 shows the size and a section, allowing for the edge of the roof, which comes next.

Fig. 4.8

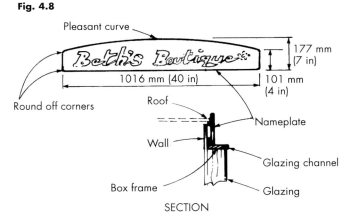

Pleasant curve

Beth's Boutique

177 mm (7 in)

1016 mm (40 in)

101 mm (4 in)

Round off corners

Roof

Nameplate

Wall

Glazing channel

Box frame

Glazing

SECTION

8 Hinge the roof panels together, before making the frame from 12 × 12 mm (½ in) strip as seen in Fig. 4.9. Note from the section, that they form a rebate to carry another styrene glazing panel, which you cut to the size of the hole in the plywood. Do not glaze until after painting.

Following Fig. 4.10, glue and pin 12 × 12 mm (½ in) strip under the ends for the roof panels. Turn

Fig. 4.9

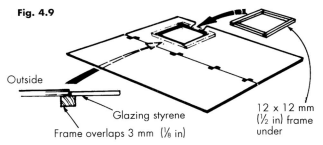

Outside

Glazing styrene

Frame overlaps 3 mm (⅛ in)

12 x 12 mm (½ in) frame under

Fig. 4.10

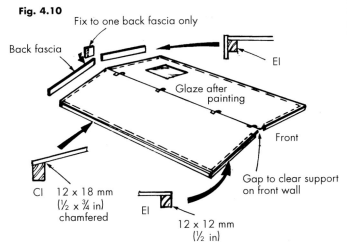

Fix to one back fascia only

Back fascia

El

Glaze after painting

Front

Gap to clear support on front wall

Cl   12 x 18 mm (½ x ¾ in) chamfered

El

12 x 12 mm (½ in)

over and clench the ends of the pins. Plane a chamfer of 15 degrees on the narrow face of two strips of 12 × 18 mm (½ × ¾ in) pine and glue and pin these under the long edges. When the roof is folded at the hinge line, it will be more rigid at the centre. Make gable strips, and a centre patch, from waste plywood. Glue and pin to the rear end only (the front edge is concealed behind the shop nameplate).

9 Cut out the floor and position the unfolded wall panels on its edges. Holding the wall panels together with G-cramps at the top corners, drill 76 mm (3 in) from top and bottom edges through the pairs of strips at the joints. Enlarge the holes to easily clear 9 mm (⅜ in) dowels in the flat strip and wall panels. Securely glue stub dowels into the edge-mounted strips. They will pass through these holes for locking and locating the pairs of walls. (See also Chapter 1 for details of this method).

10 The changing cubicle wall and counter come next. Mark out from the dimensions in Fig. 4.11 and cut them from plywood offcuts. Using the hinging technique already described, join the narrow flap and the counter support bracket to the cubicle partition, and the counter hinge flap to the counter. Glue and pin a strip of 12 × 18 mm (½ × ¾ in) pine flat to the underside front edge of the partition. It will go over the hinges already in place with the bracket. Squeeze with a G-cramp here while the glue sets, because the panel pins may not close the gap completely for a good glue bond at this point.

Fig. 4.11

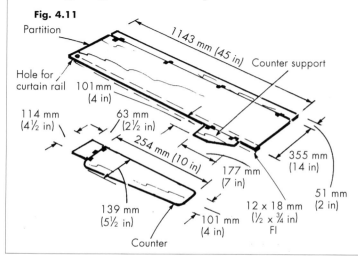

Partition
Hole for curtain rail
1143 mm (45 in)
Counter support
101 mm (4 in)
114 mm (4½ in)
63 mm (2½ in)
254 mm (10 in)
177 mm (7 in)
355 mm (14 in)
51 mm (2 in)
139 mm (5½ in)
101 mm (4 in)
12 × 18 mm (½ × ¾ in) FI
Counter

11 Fig. 4.12 shows the cubicle in position. Drill a hole at the top corner for the 9 mm (⅜ in) dowel that is to form the curtain rail. Measure its position on the back wall and drill here too.

Glue the partition flap to the side wall 406 mm (16 in) from the back wall. Swing the partition out at right angles and mark the floor at its front edge.

Fig. 4.12

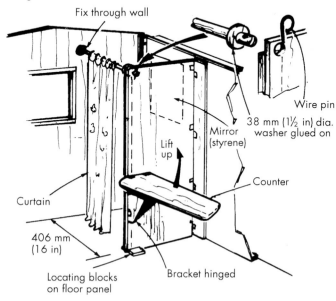

Fix through wall
Wire pin
38 mm (1½ in) dia. washer glued on
Mirror (styrene)
Lift up
Counter
Curtain
406 mm (16 in)
Locating blocks on floor panel
Bracket hinged

Glue two scraps of 12 × 18 mm (½ × ¾ in) pine here to locate it. The top corner will be secure when you install the curtain rod. This happens after you have made the curtain, and threaded its rings onto the dowel. (You have to make, and glue plywood washers at each end. These would prevent you sliding the rings on.)

Drill for coat-hanger wire locking pins about 6 mm (¼ in) outside the washers. Glue the flap of the counter hinge to the partition so that the counter rests level on the opened bracket. This whole assembly folds flat against the side wall for storage.

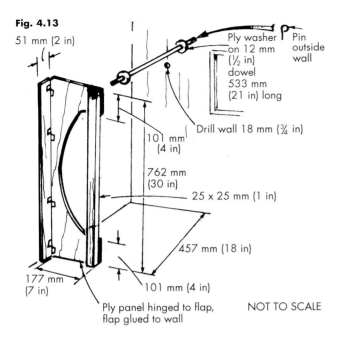

Fig. 4.13

51 mm (2 in)

Ply washer on 12 mm (½ in) dowel 533 mm (21 in) long

Pin outside wall

Drill wall 18 mm (¾ in)

101 mm (4 in)

762 mm (30 in)

25 x 25 mm (1 in)

457 mm (18 in)

177 mm (7 in)

101 mm (4 in)

Ply panel hinged to flap, flap glued to wall

NOT TO SCALE

12 Make the clothes rail support in a similar manner to the previous item. The dimensions are shown in Fig. 4.13. Drill the hole in the 12 × 18 mm (½ × ¾ in) strip for the rail; the dowel has to be 12 mm (½ in) longer between the washer and this locking-pin hole. Glue the edge strip to the left side wall. There is no need for a floor socket. The support will also fold flat for storage, when the rail is taken out.

13 No boutique is without dummies; cut two head-shaped hangers for short coats and tops to hang in the window. Use the remaining plywood offcuts for these and for the standing dummy shown in Fig. 4.14. Rather than having detachable limbs, the dummy's arms are slit well up for fitting into sleeves, and two wooden spring-type clothes pegs will grip skirts and trousers in front of the legs. Glue the bracket to the base square, but leave the slotted joint unglued, so that the foot can be taken off and the legs inserted in clothes that will not go over the dummy's head.

14 With abrasive paper, smooth away any sharp edges and corners of the boutique. Do not sand over the hinges – use filler to blend any such raised spots and to fill any hollows where pins have been clenched, and open grain areas.

Sand lightly after, then paint. Emulsion paint is fine for inside and outdoors when the weather is dry. Provided the plywood is not prone to warping when dampened on one side, you may apply small areas of wallpaper inside to brighten the walls and ceiling. Practise your brush lettering on a piece of paper, then trace it onto the painted nameplate as a guide for the proper job.

When all the paint is dry, fit the styrene glazing with hot-melt glue blobs in the skylight, and dry in the channel-section strips of the shop window, which you then glue to the bare wood front edge of the box frame. If you have painted or varnished these meeting edges before inserting the styrene

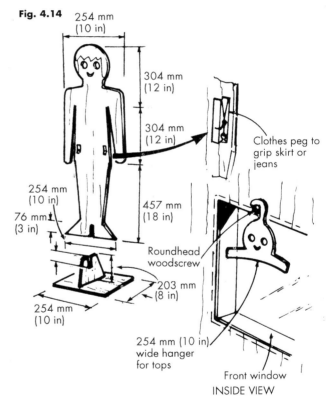

Fig. 4.14

254 mm (10 in)

304 mm (12 in)

304 mm (12 in)

Clothes peg to grip skirt or jeans

254 mm (10 in)

457 mm (18 in)

76 mm (3 in)

Roundhead woodscrew

203 mm (8 in)

254 mm (10 in)

254 mm (10 in) wide hanger for tops

254 mm (10 in) wide hanger for tops

Front window

INSIDE VIEW

panel, sand them bare ready for the glue. Also, at this time, fix the styrene mirror in the changing cubicle. Use self-adhesive pads for this, on a smooth painted area.

When storing the play-house, drape some cloth over the glazing areas to protect against scratches. If you have to clean it, do not use solvent-based polish, such as metal polish – this makes the styrene craze.

TV Studio

A natural follow-on from dressing up is acting a part. What child has not pretended to be some character on TV, or has not acted out a fantasy part of their own imagination with friends? It is all part of life's natural gift of creativity, something that needs to be catered for.

Even if there is no camcorder in the household that the older children are allowed to handle, this play-studio gives scope for being camera crew, mike-boom operator, and electrician, as well as director and actor or puppeteer. Children will revel in the use of this open-fronted studio – if not in the cast or crew, then as a studio audience.

As you can see from Fig. 5.1, the enclosure is the most economical and easiest of the projects. There is wide scope for variations to the set of accessories that are described in these instructions. They may be added to by your children's own designs and creative art, in the making of more scenery and props. You may be elected to be a second, but real camera operator from outside the front of the studio set, while the 'crew' and 'floor manager' continue to work alongside the actors.

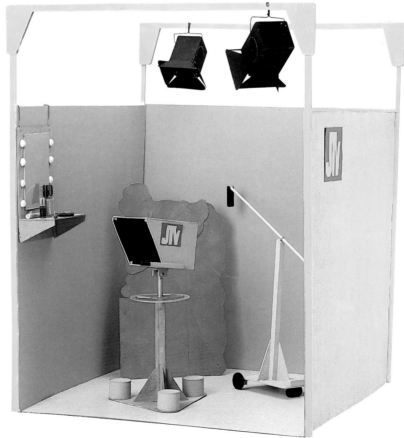

STAR RATING
Skill rating **
Cost *
Child height *****

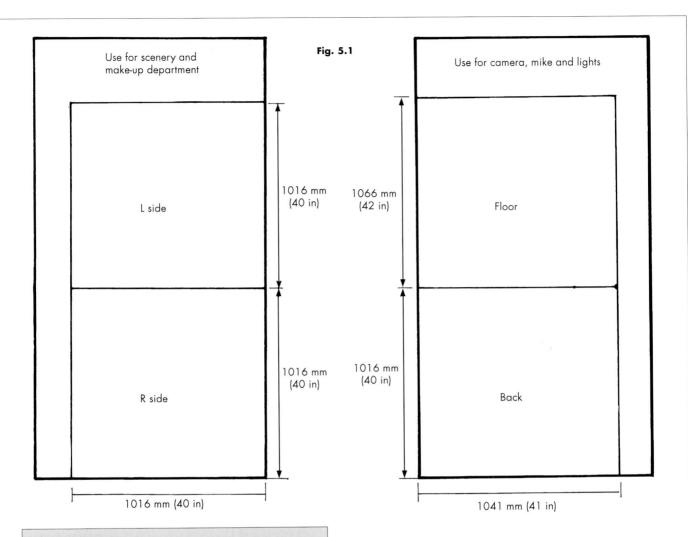

Fig. 5.1

Use for scenery and make-up department

L side

R side

1016 mm (40 in)

1016 mm (40 in)

1016 mm (40 in)

Use for camera, mike and lights

Floor

Back

1066 mm (42 in)

1016 mm (40 in)

1041 mm (41 in)

MATERIALS

4 mm (³⁄₁₆ in) plywood (or hardboard): 2 sheets 2438 × 1219 mm (8 × 4 ft)

12 × 38 mm (½ × 1½ in) pine: 2 at 152 mm (6 in)

18 × 18 mm (¾ in) pine: 3 at 508 mm (20 in)

12 × 18 mm (½ × ¾ in) pine: 4 at 1321 mm (52 in)

12 × 12 mm (½ in) pine: 4 at 1219 mm (48 in)

18 mm (¾ in) dowel: 559 mm (22 in)

9 mm (⅜ in) dowel: 1041 mm (41 in)

6 mm (¼ in) dowel: 304 mm (12 in)

Styrene mirror: 203 × 355 mm (8 × 14 in)

25 mm (1 in) strong upholstery webbing: 304 mm (12 in)

1 small castor

3 small furniture foot domes

3 empty small baked bean cans

1 large screw eye

1 small plastic bottle

The use of several pocket torches or cycle lamps

20 mm (¾ in) panel pins

Cup hooks

Masking tape

PVA glue

Glue sticks

Decorator's filler

Non-toxic paint

Coloured acetate

Thin cardboard

TOOLS

- Hand saw or hand-held circular saw
- Tenon saw
- Plane
- Screwdriver
- Drill
- Hammer
- Nail punch
- Strong pliers
- Scissors
- Glue gun
- Domestic iron
- Abrasive paper
- Pencil
- Rule
- Try square
- G-cramps
- Filling knife
- Paint brushes

Fig. 5.2

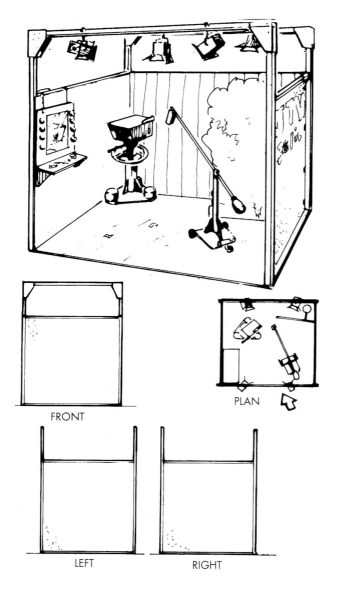

FRONT

PLAN

LEFT   RIGHT

1 For this play-house you need only two sheets of plywood, or even hardboard, for the walls and floor. The top is open, for better lighting, access and external participation. Mark out and cut the panels, as shown in Fig. 5.1. Note that the back wall is slightly longer than the sides – this is to allow for one quick-detach joint.

2 If you are using hardboard, have the smooth side on the inside of the studio. Lay the back panel smooth side up on the left, and the right panel against it, as in Fig. 5.3. Using the webbing, join them by the hinging method already described. After turning the panels over to complete the hinging sequence, leave them in this position (the back panel will now be on the left).

Fig. 5.3

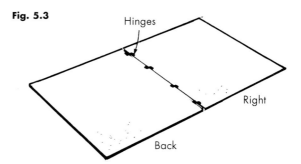

Hinges

Right

Back

3 Select strips of 12 × 18 mm (½ × ¾ in) pine, and lay them out as shown in Fig. 5.4. The longest ones will form the uprights that are to carry the top frames, so they must be strong and free from knots. One upright goes over part of the

Fig. 5.4

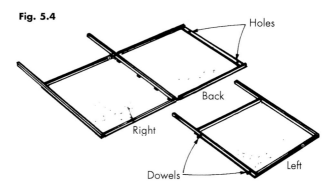

Holes

Back

Right

Left

Dowels

hinges on its own side panel. The drawing shows the finished arrangement. You have to turn the panels over while gluing and pinning the wood in place. All the framing is on the rough side (outside when you use plywood). Clench the protruding panel pin points over on the single flat-mounted strip.

TIP: GLUING AND PINNING BATTENS

The battens will be easier to fix and more accurately positioned when the panel pins are used in the order shown in the sketch. Check the opposite end after fixing at position 1, then check the centre after fixing at position 2. Fix here, then complete as shown.

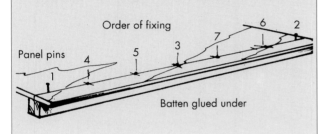

4 Drill both the edge-on and flat strips that form the joint on the outside of the enclosure (other projects have the joint inside). Fig. 5.5 explains this – the view is taken from underneath the back left corner. It is easier to understand when you have the actual panels in your hands! Until you have joined the two sides across the front and back, by plugging on the two top

Fig. 5.5

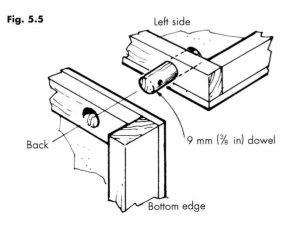

frames, they will be rather wobbly to assemble by this joint alone, so that is the next stage to complete.

5 Each frame should comprise a strong, knot-free cross bar which spaces the side panels apart. There is a socket at each end which plugs over the uprights, to hold them firmly vertical. Both frames are removable for storage.

From 4 mm (³⁄₁₆ in) plywood or good-quality hardboard, cut eight gusset pieces to the sizes shown in Fig. 5.6. Cut eight strips of 12 × 12 mm (½ in) pine to act as sides to the sockets. Check that the space between fits exactly over a spare piece of 12 × 18 mm (½ × ¾ in) pine that is identical with the tops of each upright. You will use this as a plug to form the sockets. If there is any variation, shave or sand the thickest upright to the same section as the others. The cross bars have to be the same thickness at each end too.

Fig. 5.6

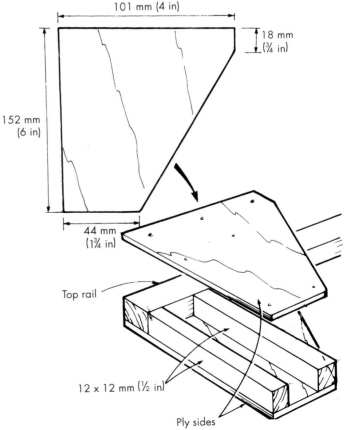

6 Glue and pin one gusset to the top piece and one outer strip. Use the try square to get it square. Lay the plug in position, push the inner strip up to it and glue and pin the gusset to that. Turn the job over and, without moving the plug, glue and pin the other gusset in place to complete the socket. Pull the plug out immediately and clean any glue from it. Now make the other three sockets in the same way.

7 If when you have finished, one frame fits better a particular way round, mark it to show where it fits. If after trying each frame on both front and back positions, left- or right-handed, you find that one upright is over-tight, trim it in easy stages. Add a sliver of wood to pack out any upright that is too loose. The frames are not supposed to be a tight fit – just sufficiently firm to prevent the uprights moving sideways.

Fig. 5.7 shows the rear frame in position. This is the first one that you put on when assembling the wall panels together. You hinge open the right-hand panel and back, so that they stand up, then with the single (left) panel in one hand and the top frame in the other, plug the frame on, and slide the back panel onto the locating dowels on the single panel. The floor fits inside the three walls.

Fig. 5.7

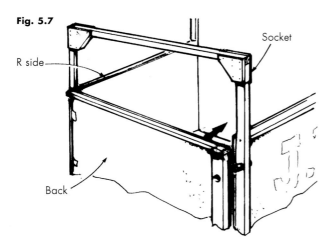

8 The make-up department is catered for by a panel and shelf with a plastic mirror and dummy lights. Two wire hooks enable it to be hung on any of the walls, inside or outside. Fig. 5.8 shows the construction and dimensions. Use plywood or hardboard, although plywood is more rigid for the shelf.

Fig. 5.8

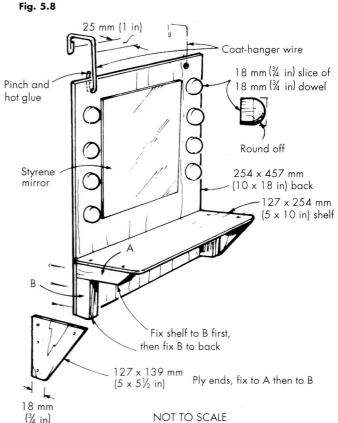

NOT TO SCALE

When you assemble it, pin and glue the shelf to the horizontal pieces of 12 × 18 mm (½ × ¾ in) strip, then the back to the vertical strips. Turn the job on its side and apply glue to the back of the shelf and its strips. Glue and pin one bracket to both strips, while supporting the latter on a corner of the bench, or on a block of wood which you clamp in position with a G-cramp. Turn the job over and do the same with the opposite bracket.

9 Using strong pliers, cut a piece of wire from a coat-hanger and form two hooks to fit over the wall panel and its edge strip. Double the top ends back so that there is no sharp edge. Drill holes at the top of the dressing room panel and pass the wires through, bend the ends over, and squeeze them tight against the back surface to lock them. You can strengthen this point with hot-melt glue to stop the hooks swivelling.

10 The dummy lights down each side of the mirror need to be rounded for realism. Start by shaving off the cut edge of a piece of 18 mm (¾ in) dowel, sand round, then saw off to length. Alternatively, saw off a short slice of dowel, tap a nail, less its head, into the centre, clamp this in the chuck of a drill and rotate it against coarse abrasive paper. If you are lucky enough to have a lathe you can do a professional job on these small items. Whichever route you choose make the surface really smooth, so that when you have painted it with white gloss it looks convincing.

11 Children will love to frame the scene by looking through the dummy TV camera, which is modelled here as a box, open at both ends. Supported on a tilt and pan head, it can be raised and lowered, and pushed around. A small torch with red acetate on the lens shows that the camera is 'live'. There are no fearsome pieces of engineering in this lightweight version.

Fig. 5.9 shows the construction and dimensions. Make the camera by gluing and pinning strips of 12 × 12 mm (½ in) strip to the inside edges of the box sides and assembling with the top and bottom, with a square frame at the back to keep it rigid. Glue and pin the corners of this, then slide it in to meet the ends of the side strips. There are no front or back panels.

12 Cut two 51 mm (2 in)-long flats on the end of a 559 mm (22 in)-long piece of 18 mm (¾ in) dowel, which is to form the support rod. Clamp a piece of 12 × 38 mm (½ × 1½ in) pine, 76 mm (3 in) long, each side on the flats, then drill right through for a piece of 6 mm (¼ in) dowel, which you should now glue into the pine pieces. This should swivel stiffly in the hole in the upright. The pine pieces should be parallel and level.

With the camera upside down, glue it fore and aft at the centre of the bottom to the swivelling support. While the glue sets, take the corners off another strip of 12 × 12 mm (½ in) strip, 254 mm

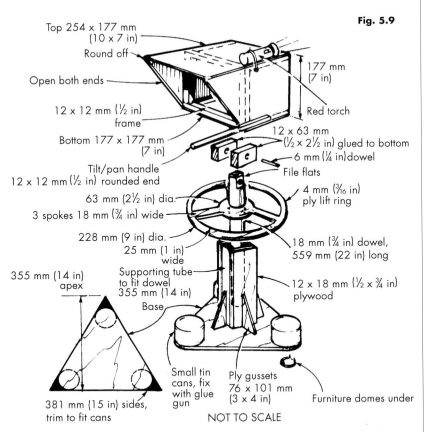

Fig. 5.9

Top 254 x 177 mm (10 x 7 in)
Round off
Open both ends
12 x 12 mm (½ in) frame
Bottom 177 x 177 mm (7 in)
Tilt/pan handle 12 x 12 mm (½ in) rounded end
63 mm (2½ in) dia.
3 spokes 18 mm (¾ in) wide
228 mm (9 in) dia.
25 mm (1 in) wide
Supporting tube to fit dowel 355 mm (14 in)
Base
355 mm (14 in) apex
381 mm (15 in) sides, trim to fit cans

177 mm (7 in)
Red torch
12 x 63 mm (½ x 2½ in) glued to bottom
6 mm (¼ in) dowel
File flats
4 mm (³⁄₁₆ in) ply lift ring
18 mm (¾ in) dowel, 559 mm (22 in) long
12 x 18 mm (½ x ¾ in) plywood
Small tin cans, fix with glue gun
Ply gussets 76 x 101 mm (3 x 4 in)
Furniture domes under
NOT TO SCALE

(10 in) long, leaving 76 mm (3 in) of it square. Glue this to the right-hand bottom edge of the camera as shown. This will be the tilt handle.

13 Cut the lift and pan wheel from 4 mm (³⁄₁₆ in) plywood and glue it onto the dowel post, 76 mm (3 in) below the flats. Reinforce the joint with a generous fillet of glue and sawdust. When dry, sand the edges of the plywood to remove any whiskers and render it comfortable to handle.

Make a supporting tube from two strips of 12 × 18 mm (½ × ¾ in) pine and strips of 4 mm (³⁄₁₆ in) plywood to fit over the dowel as shown in the illustration. The dowel should be a sliding fit, so that it grips enough to stop the camera dropping down too easily.

14 To make the triangular base, use two laminations of 4 mm (³⁄₁₆ in) plywood, with the grain of one running at right angles to the other. Glue them together under some weights while you cut four gussets from the same material. Then find three small empty baked bean cans (or similar), strip the paper away and, using hot-melt glue, fix them, open end down, onto the base.

Press or glue three furniture domes under the corners, to allow the camera to slide smoothly. Glue the support tube to the base with the gussets to support it. When in use, a foot placed on the base will restrain it while the lift wheel is pulled up to raise the camera. After painting, secure a small torch to the camera top with a rubber band through holes.

15 The microphone boom is a more simple affair. Shown and dimensioned in Fig. 5.10, it has two wheels and a castor for mobility. Rather than having a telescopic action, the wooden 'mike' moves by sliding and twisting a dowel in a screw eye.

Start by cutting a rectangle of 4 mm (³⁄₁₆ in) plywood for the base. Saw a groove in a piece of 18 × 18 mm (¾ in) pine to take a 6 mm (¼ in) dowel axle. Glue it under the front, and a second block of the same section on top at the rear into which you can mount a small castor.

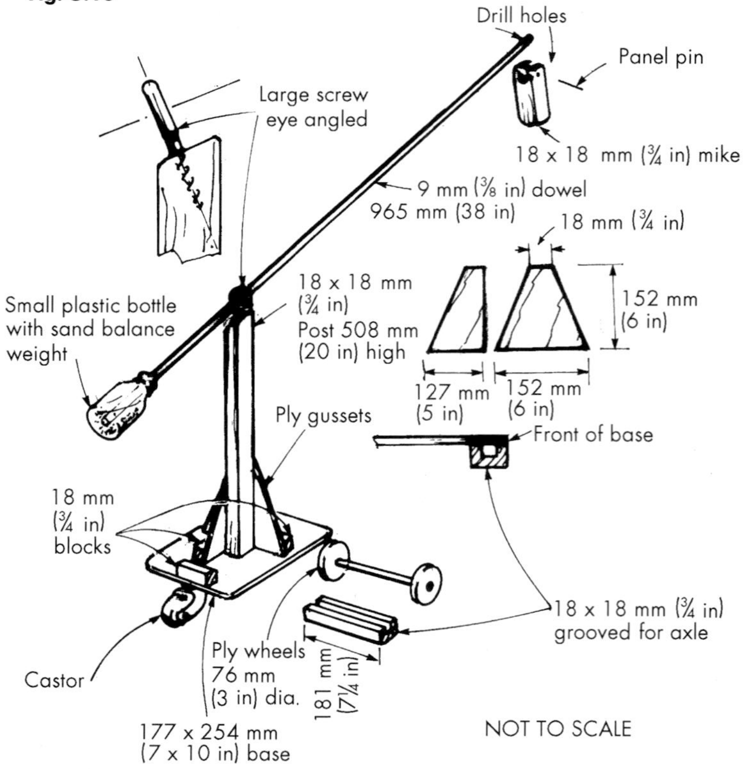

16 Saw a 30 degree chamfer at the top end of a 508 mm (20 in) piece of 18 × 18 mm (¾ in) pine. This will be the boom support post. Drill and fit a screw eye at the angle shown in Fig. 5.10, so that when in position it slopes back towards the castor. Make the gussets as shown from 4 mm (³⁄₁₆ in) plywood and fix short pieces of 18 × 18 mm (¾ in) pine to their bottom edges. Glue up this assembly on the base to support the post.

Drill a hole across the end of a 965 mm (38 in) length of 9 mm (⅜ in) dowel, which will be the boom. Slot one end of a short piece of 18 × 18 mm (¾ in) strip to form a 'mike', rounding off the corners and drilling it for a small nail to pivot it to the boom through the hole. Slide the dowel though the eyelet and into a small plastic drinks bottle, which you should fill with sand or pebbles to balance the 'mike'. Fix it there with adhesive tape or hot-melt glue.

Finally, cut out a pair of 76 mm (3 in) dia. wheels from the plywood, using either a jigsaw or a hole saw (the latter will leave a central hole to fit the dowel axle). Glue on one wheel, slide the axle through the grooved strip and glue on the other wheel.

17 Make four or more simple boxes that are to represent the studio lights – they are shown in Fig. 5.11. Use a strip of 12 × 12 mm (½ in) pine in each corner. All the panels are identical, lap one over the previous one when you glue them. Hold them with masking tape rather than panel pins.

With pliers, bend up coat-hanger wire to form supporting hooks. Bind the wire together with adhesive tape for rigidity, as shown. Spring the ends into a couple of centrally positioned holes in the sides of the boxes. If you put a panel pin in the end of each corner strip you can hook elastic bands over them to carry small torches for lighting the scene. The 'doors' which these full-size lights have, give them character. Model them here with pieces of thin cardboard, glued on so that the children can adjust then when 'lighting' the set.

Fig. 5.10

Drill holes
Panel pin
Large screw eye angled
18 x 18 mm (¾ in) mike
9 mm (⅜ in) dowel 965 mm (38 in)
18 mm (¾ in)
152 mm (6 in)
Small plastic bottle with sand balance weight
18 x 18 mm (¾ in)
Post 508 mm (20 in) high
Ply gussets
127 mm (5 in)
152 mm (6 in)
Front of base
18 mm (¾ in) blocks
18 x 18 mm (¾ in) grooved for axle
Castor
Ply wheels 76 mm (3 in) dia.
181 mm (7¼ in)
177 x 254 mm (7 x 10 in) base
NOT TO SCALE

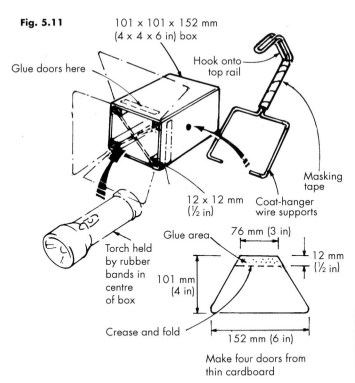

Fig. 5.11

101 x 101 x 152 mm (4 x 4 x 6 in) box

Glue doors here

Hook onto top rail

Masking tape

12 x 12 mm (½ in)

Coat-hanger wire supports

Torch held by rubber bands in centre of box

Glue area

76 mm (3 in)

12 mm (½ in)

101 mm (4 in)

152 mm (6 in)

Crease and fold

Make four doors from thin cardboard

18 Pieces of scenery help to complete the set. You can make basic pieces from hardboard or thick cardboard as shown in Fig. 5.12. You need a basic support, which you can make from more 12 × 18 mm (½ × ¾ in) strip and add a plywood

gusset and platform on which to place a weight. Bend two cup hooks so that they lean out at about 45 degrees and fit into holes in whatever piece of scenery they have to support. The same piece of hardboard or cardboard can be painted differently on the back and turned before hooking it on. With a little ingenuity, the children can use the mirror outline of one piece to show either the back of the same subject, or something quite different.

19 Sand any remaining rough edges of the studio and equipment. Fill hollows and smoothly blend any necessary raised areas, sand lightly and paint. You can design and paint a studio logo on the outside of the panels. Emulsion paint is best, so that the lights, within or on a camcorder, do not reflect.

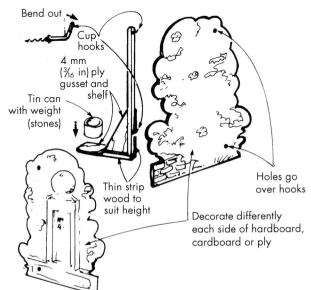

Fig. 5.12

Bend out

Cup hooks

4 mm (³⁄₁₆ in) ply gusset and shelf

Tin can with weight (stones)

Thin strip wood to suit height

Holes go over hooks

Decorate differently each side of hardboard, cardboard or ply

TIP: STRAIGHT CUTS

If you must use a hand saw or panel saw, have the plywood on a deep enough piece of supporting wood on the floor. Hold the saw at a shallow angle and make short strokes. Do not exert too much pressure, or the underside of the plywood will have distressed grain. The panels are quite large, and by working on the floor, you avoid the plywood twisting and probably breaking near narrow areas. Some people lean the panel against a wall or doorway, but this often allows the wood to vibrate and there is even more risk of damage due to its weight. If you have to do these tricks, clamp the wood to a a supporting batten above the area of cutting.

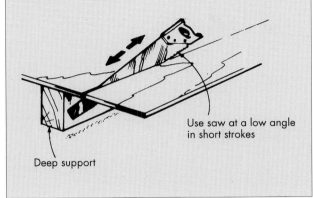

Use saw at a low angle in short strokes

Deep support

Garage

There may already be a toy car in the household, but this play-house project also has its own vintage-style vehicle. This can be put up on jacks and the wheels removed and changed around. There is a workbench, too. Outside there is a petrol pump and an air supply station. Double doors and two windows let in plenty of light, and the owner can add plenty of oddments and tools to complete the scene shown in Fig. 6.1.

The enclosure is compact at 1016 mm (40 in) square, and a full 1219 mm (48 in) high at the ridge of its shallow pitched roof. There is a wealth of play possibilities here. The car can be trundled out, even though, for simplicity, it does not steer. It is, however, so light, that its driver can change direction by skidding the front across.

STAR RATING
Skill rating ***
Cost ***
Child height ****

MATERIALS

4 mm (³⁄₁₆ in) plywood:
  3 sheets 2438 ×
  1219 mm (8 × 4 ft)
6 mm (¼ in) plywood:
  half sheet, door size, or
  609 × 1219 mm
  (2 × 4 ft), whichever is
  smaller
44 × 44 mm (1¾ in) pine:
  3 at 508 mm (20 in)
12 × 38 mm (½ × 1½ in)
  pine: 1 at 1219 mm
  (48 in)
  1 at 660 mm (26 in)
12 × 18 mm (½ × ¾ in)
  pine: 5 at 1092 mm
  (43 in)
  2 at 1066 mm (42 in)
  10 at 1016 mm (40 in)
12 × 12 mm (½ in) pine:
  3 at 762 mm (30 in)
  5 at 508 mm (20 in)
12 mm (½ in) hardwood
  dowel: 762 mm (30 in)

9 mm (⅜ in) hardwood
  dowel: 254 mm (10 in)
6 mm (¼ in) hardwood
  dowel: 304 mm (12 in)
25 mm (1 in)-wide strong
  upholstery webbing:
  1676 mm (66 in)
2 small plastic cups
  (or yoghurt pots)
Short piece of plastic
  covered clothes-line
9 mm (⅜ in) soft plastic
  tube: 1.5 m (1½ yd)
Miniature portable vice
5 at 51 mm (2 in) no. 8
  countersunk woodscrews
20 mm (¾ in) panel pins
PVA glue
Glue sticks
Filler
Non-toxic paint
Small amount of gloss
  varnish

TOOLS

- Hand saw or hand-held
  circular saw
- Tenon saw
- Hand-held jigsaw
- Plane
- Chisel
- Drill
- Hole saw
- Screwdriver
- Hammer
- Nail punch
- Scissors
- Glue gun
- Domestic iron
- Abrasive paper
- Sander
- Pencil
- Rule
- Compass
- Try square
- G-cramps
- Filling knife
- Paint brushes

1 Mark out the three sheets of plywood for the main play-house components. The areas left will provide some of the material for the accessories.

Using the hand-held circular saw for preference, make the long straight cuts first, so as not to divide the surplus areas of plywood into any smaller pieces than you see in Fig. 6.2. Work on a

Fig. 6.1

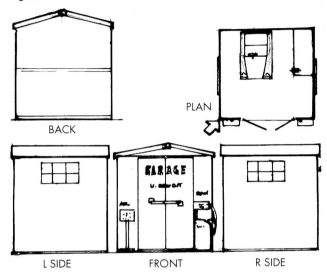

BACK   PLAN

L SIDE   FRONT   R SIDE

GARGE

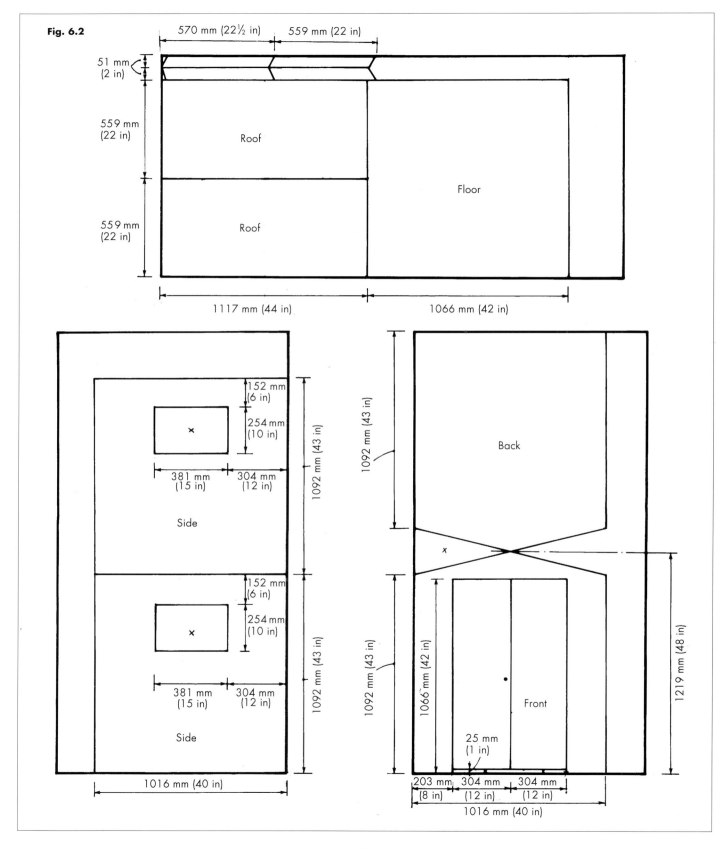

Fig. 6.2

570 mm (22½ in)   559 mm (22 in)

51 mm (2 in)

559 mm (22 in)

Roof

Floor

559 mm (22 in)

Roof

1117 mm (44 in)   1066 mm (42 in)

152 mm (6 in)

254 mm (10 in)

1092 mm (43 in)

381 mm (15 in)   304 mm (12 in)

Side

152 mm (6 in)

254 mm (10 in)

1092 mm (43 in)

381 mm (15 in)   304 mm (12 in)

Side

1016 mm (40 in)

1092 mm (43 in)

Back

1092 mm (43 in)

1219 mm (48 in)

1066 mm (42 in)

Front

25 mm (1 in)

203 mm (8 in)   304 mm (12 in)   304 mm (12 in)

1016 mm (40 in)

48

level floor, with a piece of thick-section wood underneath close to the intended cutting line. This will space the sheet of plywood clear enough to allow the saw blade and its cover to clear the floor. Join up cuts made to the top of the doors with the jigsaw, inserted via a hole drilled at one top corner. Treat the window openings in a similar way, by drilling two holes, one diagonal to the other. Insert the jigsaw blade in one to make two right-angled cuts, then cut from the other hole to meet them. Keep all the cut pieces flat until needed, so that they do not warp. Mark each to identify it and show which side is outermost. The cutting plan in Fig. 6.2 is drawn to show the outsides.

2 Pairs of panels will support each other when you hinge them together, so following Fig. 6.3, lay out the walls and doors on the floor. With scissors, cut 32 pieces of webbing, each 38 mm (1½ in) long and lay them in pairs along the hinge lines shown.

Using the glue gun, fix one half of each pair to the left side and one half of its partner to the right. The glue does not have to cover the entire half of each piece of webbing. After gluing all the pieces, press them flat with the domestic iron set to full heat. This remelts the glue, and draws it into the weave of the webbing to strengthen the bond. Hold the free end of the webbing to prevent it skidding.

3 You now have half the hinges on one side of each panel. Turn the panels over, and as you do, wipe the hinges with the iron so that they lean around the edges. As the panels go down, the hinges will stick up between, leaning alternately towards their opposite sides.

Fix these free ends first with the glue gun, then with the iron, as you did initially. Check that no hinge is doubled back over onto the same side! You can rectify mistakes by reironing. Drag hot areas into place with a scrap of wood: pointed implements will unravel the webbing.

4 The panels will need to be made more rigid, so tackle one hinged pair at a time. Following Fig. 6.4, glue and pin strips of 12 × 18 mm (½ × ¾ in) pine where shown, remembering to turn the hinged assemblies over to their original sides, of course. Note which strips are laid flat, and which are on edge. The key diagrams and identity letters serve as a reminder. Fix all those strips that are underneath (inside face) first. One edge-on strip has to be set back by its own thickness from the edge, this is part of the joining corner.

Turn the panels over and fix all the outside strips. Stack the work so that it is warp free, while you hinge and finish the roof.

Fig. 6.3

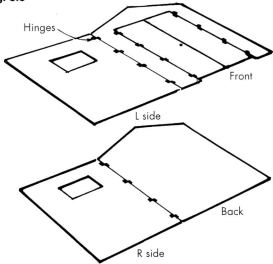

Fig. 6.4

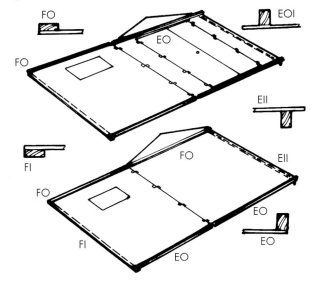

Fig. 6.5

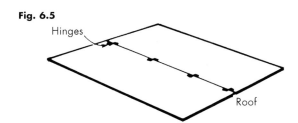

5 Fig. 6.5 shows the positions of the hinges, which you now fix as before. The roof gains rigidity when you fold it to a slight angle, so it only needs stiffening strips at the edges.

Glue and pin a strip of 12 × 12 mm (½ in) pine at the end edges of the panels, as shown in Fig. 6.6. Turn the panels over and clench the points down. Take two strips of 12 × 18 mm (½ × ¾ in) pine and plane one narrow edge of each to a 15 degree chamfer. If you draw a guideline 3 mm (⅛ in) down on the wide face, it will help.

When you glue and pin these with their chamfered edge against the panels, pack the ridge up so that the panels seat at the correct angle on the strips. The strip then sits square on its level bottom edge, and you can drive the panel pins in without rocking it. Put one pin at each end first, then at the centre, and work outwards. When the end strips have set, turn the roof on end, and fix the gable pieces on. Glue the centre cover squares to one gable piece only, at each end of the roof. This will allow the roof to be hinged up and over for storage.

Fig. 6.6

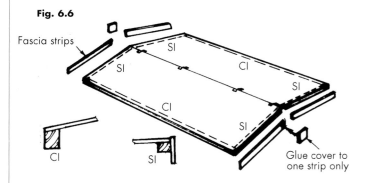

6 This project has glazing bars in the window frames. Fig. 6.7 shows the detail. With a tenon saw or a plough plane (if you have one), form a shallow groove for the panel edge in strips of 12 × 12 mm (½ in) pine. Avoid knots in all the window strips. Glue the top and bottom strips in first, then

Fig. 6.7

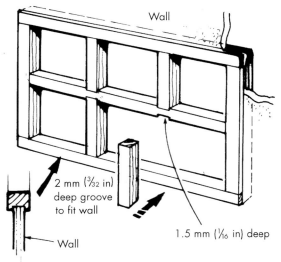

add the sides. Measure carefully for the horizontal bar, and try it for fit before you form shallow housings for the vertical bars. Lay a try square against these to ensure that they do not lean.

The walls are now complete, so bring the joint corners together, clamp them and drill through the joint strips 76 mm (3 in) from top and bottom. Insert and glue in the 9 mm (⅜ in) dowel pegs which form the quick-detach fixings. (See Chapter 1.)

Fig. 6.8

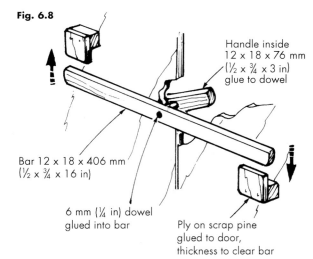

7 The doors are secured with a swing-over locking bar, as shown in Fig. 6.8. A 406 mm (16 in) length of 12 × 18 mm (½ × ¾ in) pine is pivoted near the open edge of the left-hand door. In the vertical position, it clears both doors and allows them to swing in or out. Pivot this, and a shorter piece (which forms a handle inside), on a short piece of 6 mm (¼ in) dowel. The hole in the door should be a free fit, whilst those in the strips have to be tight, for gluing.

Make two sockets from plywood and short spacer pieces of 12 × 18 mm (½ × ¾ in) scrap pine. Sand the ends of the locking bar to make it a fraction thinner than the spacers, turn the bar horizontal and glue one socket facing up and the other facing down, onto the doors, over the ends of the bar.

8 The air pump is to the left of the doors, fixed to the front panel. Fig. 6.9 shows the construction. Glue the 12 × 38 mm (½ × 1½ in) pine strips to form a box on the back of the small panel. Round off the narrow face of a strip of 12 × 18 mm (½ × ¾ in) pine and glue it above a short piece of the wider strip to the front wall. Glue the finished box on top, adding a length of clothes line as the air line. Paint the face to represent a pressure dial.

9 The petrol pump goes to the right of the doors. Make two boxes in the same manner as the air pump – the sizes are shown in Fig. 6.10. You have to chamfer the ends of three strips on the lower box. Cut the slot after fixing them – it should be just wider than 8 mm (under ⅜ in).

Cut the pump nozzle from plywood and add a short doubler to the spout, to hook into the slot. Cut a slot in the other end and glue in a short piece of 9 mm (⅜ in) dowel. Plug this into the plastic tube and fix the free end of the latter into a hole in the top box, using a piece of dowel inside the tube to form a wedge.

Glue the two boxes to the front wall with a strip of 12 × 18 mm (½ × ¾ in) pine between. Paint the top box to represent the meter numbers, and paint a logo on the bottom part.

Fig. 6.10

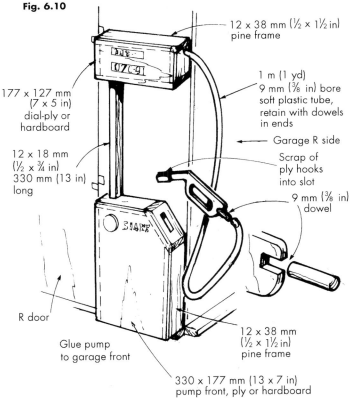

12 x 38 mm (½ x 1½ in) pine frame

1 m (1 yd) 9 mm (⅜ in) bore soft plastic tube, retain with dowels in ends

177 x 127 mm (7 x 5 in) dial-ply or hardboard

Garage R side

Scrap of ply hooks into slot

12 x 18 mm (½ x ¾ in) 330 mm (13 in) long

9 mm (⅜ in) dowel

R door

Glue pump to garage front

12 x 38 mm (½ x 1½ in) pine frame

330 x 177 mm (13 x 7 in) pump front, ply or hardboard

Fig. 6.9

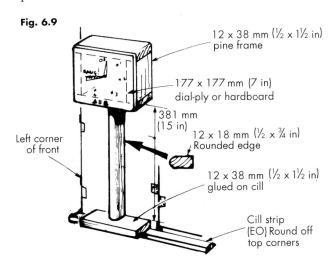

12 x 38 mm (½ x 1½ in) pine frame

177 x 177 mm (7 in) dial-ply or hardboard

381 mm (15 in)

12 x 18 mm (½ x ¾ in) Rounded edge

12 x 38 mm (½ x 1½ in) glued on cill

Left corner of front

Cill strip (EO) Round off top corners

10 The workbench inside is a more solid job, to take some hammering. Start by making the front legs and rail, as in Fig. 6.11 The halving joints are easy to make. Mark the width of one

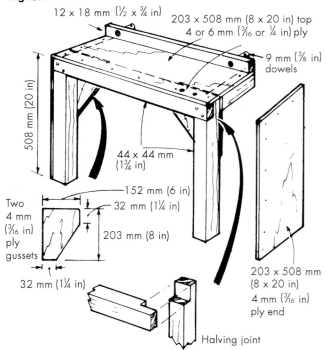

Fig. 6.11

12 x 18 mm (½ x ¾ in)

203 x 508 mm (8 x 20 in) top
4 or 6 mm (³⁄₁₆ or ¼ in) ply

9 mm (³⁄₈ in) dowels

508 mm (20 in)

44 x 44 mm (1¾ in)

Two 4 mm (³⁄₁₆ in) ply gussets

152 mm (6 in)

32 mm (1¼ in)

203 mm (8 in)

32 mm (1¼ in)

203 x 508 mm (8 x 20 in)

4 mm (³⁄₁₆ in) ply end

Halving joint

piece of 44 × 44 mm (1¾ in) pine on the other, then draw a line half the thickness, to show the size of the recess which you cut with the tenon saw. Make the first cut lengthwise, with the job upright in a vice, then saw across to meet the first cut. Both pieces should fit flush.

Glue and screw the joints to form an inverted 'U', then make a pair of gussets from plywood. Glue and pin one on the back of each joint.

11 Cut the bench top from the 6 mm (¼ in) plywood (thinner material would be too pliable). Glue and pin it to the front frame, and cut more 44 × 44 mm (1¾ in) pine to go under each end, butted up to the gussets. Support these underneath, and glue and pin the top onto them. Make a pair of 4 mm (³⁄₁₆ in) ply ends, and glue and pin these to the legs and top pieces, just fixed.

The bench needs a fixing to the wall, so drill a strip of 12 × 18 mm (½ × ¾ in) pine to take 9 mm (³⁄₈ in) dowels, which you glue in firmly. Offer the bench up to the back corner of the side wall, mark for the dowel holes and drill. Push the bench up tight and mark the dowels for drilling a hole for coat-hanger wire locking pegs in each.

You can complete the scene by fitting a small screw-on bench vice at the front corner, but this is optional. Now for the car.

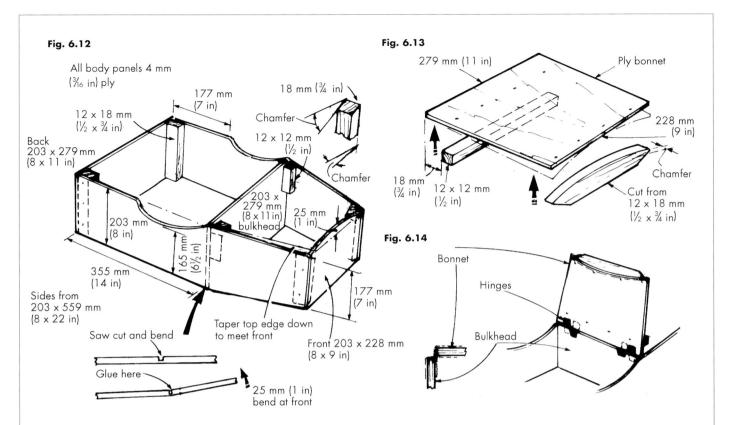

Fig. 6.12

All body panels 4 mm (³⁄₁₆ in) ply

177 mm (7 in)

12 × 18 mm (½ × ¾ in)

Back 203 × 279 mm (8 × 11 in)

18 mm (¾ in)

Chamfer

12 × 12 mm (½ in)

Chamfer

203 × 279 mm (8 × 11 in) bulkhead

25 mm (1 in)

203 mm (8 in)

165 mm (6½ in)

355 mm (14 in)

Sides from 203 × 559 mm (8 × 22 in)

Saw cut and bend

Glue here

Taper top edge down to meet front

177 mm (7 in)

Front 203 × 228 mm (8 × 9 in)

25 mm (1 in) bend at front

Fig. 6.13

279 mm (11 in)

Ply bonnet

228 mm (9 in)

18 mm (¾ in)

12 × 12 mm (½ in)

Chamfer

Cut from 12 × 18 mm (½ × ¾ in)

Fig. 6.14

Bonnet

Hinges

Bulkhead

12 Start by marking out and cutting the 4 mm (³⁄₁₆ in) ply offcut areas to form the car body. The dimensions are shown in Fig. 6.12. You have to cut almost fully through the sides from inside, so that they bend inward slightly. Be sure to mark them out left- and right-handed before doing this. Glue and pin the corners with strips of 12 × 18 mm (½ × ¾ in) pine to reinforce the joints, slide the central division down at the slotted point and add a glue fillet each side. You should slightly chamfer the front strips to accept the side taper, and on the top ends for clearance.

13 Make the bonnet lid with the more flexible grain direction to aid curving, as shown in Fig. 6.13. Set the shaped front strip back to fit inside the radiator front, and the back strip forward, clear of where you are to put hinges. This is one component that you hinge *after* adding the wood strips. Fix two pairs of webbing hinges while the bonnet is raised to the same line as the dividing panel (see Fig. 6.14). Close the bonnet, trimming the front strip if necessary to get a firm closure, but not so tight as to be hard to open.

14 Add more strip to the inside to support a seat, as in Fig. 6.15, and to wedge out a pair of front axle doublers, which are detailed in Fig. 6.16. The reason for these is that the tapered sides would not make a level surface next to the two spacing washers, which you glue to the front axle when it is in place. These prevent the front wheels rubbing on the sides.

Fig. 6.15

Seat 177 × 279 mm (7 × 11 in)

Notch corners

Chamfer

70 mm (2¾ in)

12 × 18 mm (½ × ¾ in) seat rails

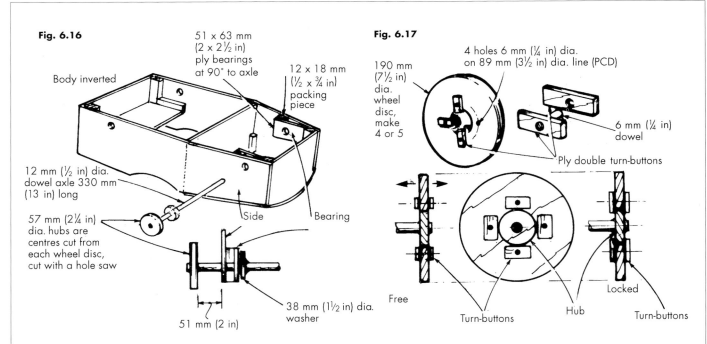

Fig. 6.16

Body inverted

51 x 63 mm (2 x 2½ in) ply bearings at 90° to axle

12 x 18 mm (½ x ¾ in) packing piece

12 mm (½ in) dia. dowel axle 330 mm (13 in) long

57 mm (2¼ in) dia. hubs are centres cut from each wheel disc, cut with a hole saw

Side

Bearing

51 mm (2 in)

38 mm (1½ in) dia. washer

Fig. 6.17

190 mm (7½ in) dia. wheel disc, make 4 or 5

4 holes 6 mm (¼ in) dia. on 89 mm (3½ in) dia. line (PCD)

6 mm (¼ in) dowel

Ply double turn-buttons

Free

Turn-buttons

Hub

Locked

Turn-buttons

15 The wheel hubs are glued to the axle. Make four wheels with integral hubs from 6 mm (¼ in) plywood. Mark out the full diameter with a compass and then drill out the centre using a 6 mm (¼ in) bit. Cut out the wheel to the outside diameter, place it on a piece of dowel in the vice and rotate against a sander or sanding block held rigidly against a bench stop or the edge of the bench. This trues up the edge.

The hole in the centre of the wheel will take the pilot drill of the hole saw, which you now use to form the hub from the wheel centre itself to ensure concentricity. Open out the centre hole to fit the axle, first using a countersink then a larger drill. Glue each hub to the axle, when the latter is in the body, allowing a fraction to project for a fillet of glue on the outside as well as the inside. Use the try square to check that the hubs are wobble-free.

16 The wheels can be reversed to expose their inner sides, which you can paint a different colour. They are clamped to the hubs with double turn-buttons, which you make according to Fig. 6.17. Cut 32 rectangles from waste 4 mm (³⁄₁₆ in) plywood, and round off the corners. Drill each centrally 6 mm (¼ in). Cut 16 pieces of 6 mm (¼ in) dowel, each 18 mm (¾ in) long. Glue one end of each into a rectangle and let it set. Drill four holes in the wheel as shown. They should be half

the width of a rectangle from the edge of the hub. The dowels should turn easily in them, but should not be a sloppy fit. Now glue the remaining rectangles to each dowel when it protrudes through the wheel. These turn-buttons should be flat against the wheel faces, so the dowel will not be flush outside. Run a bead of glue around the dowel for reinforcement. When the turn-buttons are all turned clear of the edge of the hole, you can put the wheel onto the hub. Twist the turn-buttons 90 degrees to lock the wheel in four places. Wheels can be taken off and changed around by using a wooden spanner on the buttons, or by hand.

17 With the wheels in place to check clearance, you can make and fit the wings (mudguards). Fig. 6.18 shows the dimensions of the strip of 4 mm (³⁄₁₆ in) plywood which you will separate to make it crank over at each end. Sand a chamfer in the ends of the four sloping pieces. Apply PVA glue to the inner edges, leaving a small gap at the end of each piece. Put a dab of hot-melt glue there as you press each piece against the side of the body; this will hold the components steady while the PVA sets. Finish off with PVA glue fillets both sides of the joints. Headlights are optional – if desired, small plastic cups or yoghurt pots can represent them. Fix to both wing and bonnet side with hot-melt glue.

Fig. 6.18

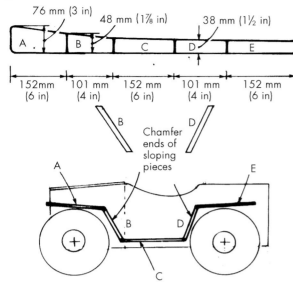

76 mm (3 in)   48 mm (1⅞ in)   38 mm (1½ in)

A   B   C   D   E

152mm (6 in)   101 mm (4 in)   152 mm (6 in)   101 mm (4 in)   152 mm (6 in)

Chamfer ends of sloping pieces

18 Make a windscreen frame from three pieces of 4 mm (³⁄₁₆ in) plywood (see Fig. 6.19). Cut the main piece with the outer grain across and the side doublers with the grain vertical. Glue these on the back face to stiffen it, then sand the top end of the doublers to blend with the main frame. Glue the screen to the body divider, which now becomes a dashboard. When the glue has set, sand the edges, because the screen will get used as a handle to heave the car about.

Fig. 6.19

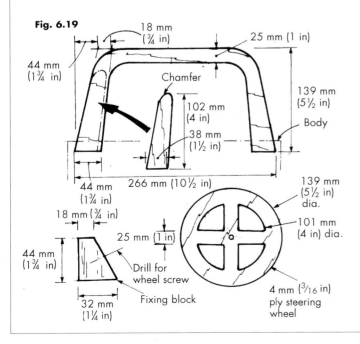

18 mm (¾ in)   25 mm (1 in)

44 mm (1¾ in)

Chamfer

102 mm (4 in)

38 mm (1½ in)

139 mm (5½ in)

Body

44 mm (1¾ in)   266 mm (10½ in)

139 mm (5½ in) dia.

18 mm (¾ in)

25 mm (1 in)

44 mm (1¾ in)

Drill for wheel screw

Fixing block

32 mm (1¼ in)

101 mm (4 in) dia.

4 mm (³⁄₁₆ in) ply steering wheel

Fig. 6.20

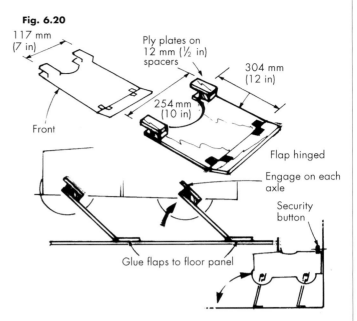

117 mm (7 in)

Ply plates on 12 mm (½ in) spacers

304 mm (12 in)

254 mm (10 in)

Front

Flap hinged

Engage on each axle

Security button

Glue flaps to floor panel

Cut the steering wheel from the same material and mount it on a woodscrew to a chamfered block of pine offcut. Glue this to the divider, clear of the windscreen.

19 Fig. 6.20 shows how to make a car-lift or jack: the car can be jacked up at either or both ends by pushing it over one or both of the hinged brackets that you will have hinged and glued to the garage floor, in line with both axles.

Lift up each and roll the car back to hook its axles on, then push back and it will rise up and rest against the back wall. It can be locked there with a turn-button or hook, to prevent it dropping forward and down (this exercise is not for tiny tots).

20 After a final clean up, fill and sand, paint the garage a dirty white inside and any not-too-gaudy colour outside. The doors can be glossy in a strong colour, with dirty finger marks at the opening edges and around the locking bar. Do some lettering as appropriate for the owner's name. Pick out the pumps for petrol and air in bright colours, and make the car colourful but with black tyres. Paint all the turn-buttons and hubs silver, with a different colour on the back of the wheel centres to that on the outside. Paint several oily coloured puddles on the floor, and gloss varnish them for realism. You might make a cobweb out of thread and fix it in a window, just to add more atmosphere.

Shop

Old village shops, the kind where you can buy everything from a lawn-mower to groceries, can be fascinating places. Young minds have no boundaries when it comes to what you can buy in a particular shop. The shop changes to suit. So this old bow-fronted project adapts readily, and carries with it the atmosphere of proper personal customer service – no check-outs here! Users can be shopkeeper or customer at will. The small pane oriel bay has a narrow shelf and space behind for boxes of goods. The shop nameplate looks antique, and the little side window has hinged shutters. At the back there is a counter with storage space and a flap, and more goods are displayed on the wall behind.

Inside the play-house, the occupants are cut off from other household distractions, in a world of their own that is environmentally sympathetic to their play theme. Fig. 7.1 shows how the compact arrangement assembles. It is 1016 mm (40 in) square and 1219 mm (48 in) high at the ridge. The door is 1066 mm (42 in) high. The play-house folds up to occupy a floor space of about 1016 × 203 mm (40 × 8 in).

STAR RATING
Skill level **
Cost ***
Child height *****

MATERIALS

4 mm (³⁄₁₆ in) plywood:
3 sheets 2438 ×
1219 mm (8 × 4 ft)
12 × 63 mm (½ × 2½ in)
pine: 152 mm (6 in)
12 × 18 mm (½ × ¾ in)
pine: 5 at 1066 mm
(42 in)
8 at 1016 mm (40 in)
2 at 736 mm (29 in)
2 at 559 mm (22 in)
12 × 12 mm (½ in) pine:
2 at 1117 mm (44 in)
3 at 1041 mm (41 in)
4 at 660 mm (26 in)
Narrow strip of Formica
or similar plastic
laminate (offcut)

9 mm (⅜ in) hardwood
dowel: 304 mm (12 in)
6 mm (¼ in) hardwood
dowel: 457 mm (18 in)
25 mm (1 in)-wide strong
upholstery webbing:
1371 mm (54 in)
Coat-hanger wire
20 mm (¾ in) panel pins
1 small screw eye
Thin rubber bands
Waste cardboard
PVA glue
Glue sticks
Abrasive paper
Decorator's filler
Non-toxic paint

TOOLS

- Hand saw or hand-held circular saw
- Tenon saw
- Hand-held jigsaw
- Plane
- Chisel
- Hammer
- Nail punch
- Drill
- Hot-melt glue gun

- Domestic iron
- Strong pliers
- G-cramps
- Sanding block
- Filling knife
- Paint brushes
- Pencil
- Rule
- Try square

Fig. 7.1

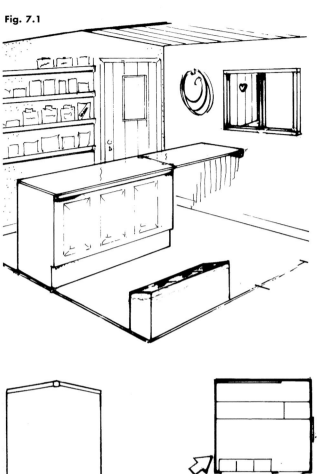

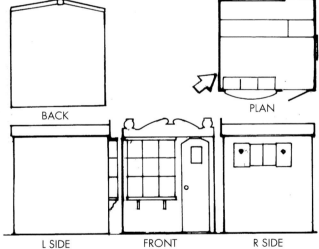

BACK   PLAN

L SIDE   FRONT   R SIDE

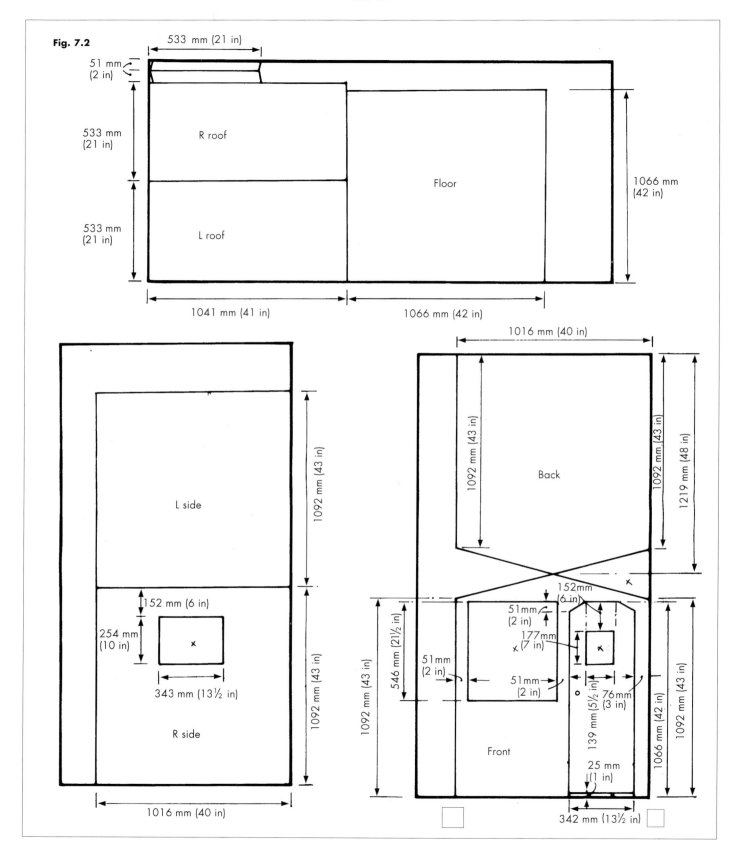

Fig. 7.2

1 Lay the plywood sheets on the floor one at a time, and mark them out according to Fig. 7.2. Then, with a thick packing piece underneath, close to the line, saw into the panel shapes. Where there is a window or door, complete these cuts before storing the pieces flat, ready for use. Drill a hole to start each jigsaw cut. You need one hole at the top of the door to join straight cuts made with the saw, and two in each window (diagonal corners). Mark each piece of the outer face (shown in Fig. 7.2).

2 Pairs of panels and doors are hinged, as in Fig. 7.3. Work flat on the floor and cut 24 pieces of webbing each 38 mm (1½ in) long. Position them in evenly spaced pairs, then using the glue gun attach one half of each alternately to left and right. Iron flat with the domestic iron, which completes the bond. Turn all the pieces over and make the webbing ends lean over the edges with the iron. Once down on the floor, they will point to their opposite panel. Repeat the fixing method to finish this set.

Fig. 7.4

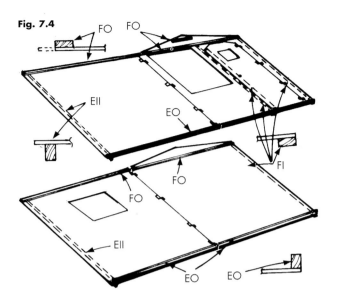

Fig. 7.3

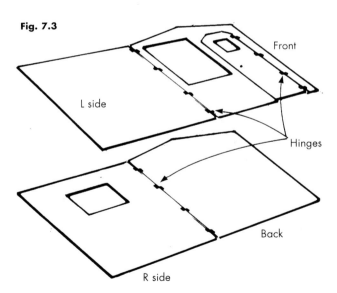

3 Glue and pin the edge strips, which are all 12 × 18 mm (½ × ¾ in) pine, to the panels where shown in Fig. 7.4. Do those on the back faces first, when the panels are outer-side up. Slide the packing piece under to support each firmly, one at a time down the whole length. Put a panel pin in at each end, then at the centre, before the rest. Clench the points of those that go through the flat strips before continuing. Note which are on

edge, and that two are inset from the edge for making the quick-detach joints.

4 The front panel will finish up face downwards. You can allow the side panel to lean against a wall if you are short of space. Slide the packing piece under the bottom of the window. Glue and pin on small pieces of 12 × 12 mm (½ in) strip along the edge, as in Fig. 7.5.

Now turn the packing around and fix a strip of 12 × 18 mm (½ × ¾ in) pine on edge, up each side, to within 4 mm (³⁄₁₆ in) of the long top strip. While the glue sets, cut top and bottom plywood pieces from some of the offcuts to the dimensions in the same figure.

Fig. 7.5

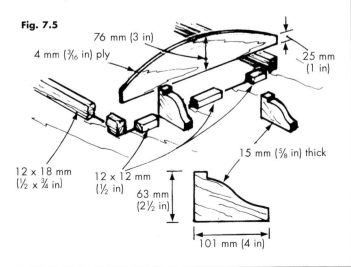

5 From the small piece of 12 × 63 mm (½ × 2½ in) pine, cut two brackets, using the jigsaw. Turn the wall panel over and glue the bottom piece of plywood to the blocks and brackets to form the window-shelf. Glue and pin the top piece under the long strip over the opening, as in Fig. 7.6. Support the strip with a heavy piece of wood or a mallet where you are working here. You now have a curved oriel window frame.

Fig. 7.6

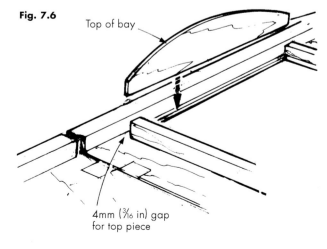

Top of bay

4mm (³⁄₁₆ in) gap for top piece

6 Cut two strips of 12 × 12 mm (½ in) pine to fit between top and bottom plywood pieces (see Fig. 7.7). Fix each with glue and a panel pin into each end. Cut two 25 mm (1 in)-wide edging strips from plywood with the outer grain across, so that they are flexible (or use hardboard). Glue and pin these along the curved edges with an overlap at each edge (see the section). Now cut more strips of 12 × 12 mm (½ in) pine for the horizontal bars. Measure two to fit between the upright bars and four to go between those and the side strips, all as shown in Fig. 7.7. Note that these last strips have notched ends, which you cut to fit as you go.

Fig. 7.8

127 mm (5 in) dia.

203 mm (8 in)

139 mm (5½ in)

70 mm (2¾ in)

Nameplate from 203 × 1016 mm (8 × 40 in) plywood

Spacer

Fascia

Batten

Wall

SECTION

Top piece

Cap strip

Fig. 7.7

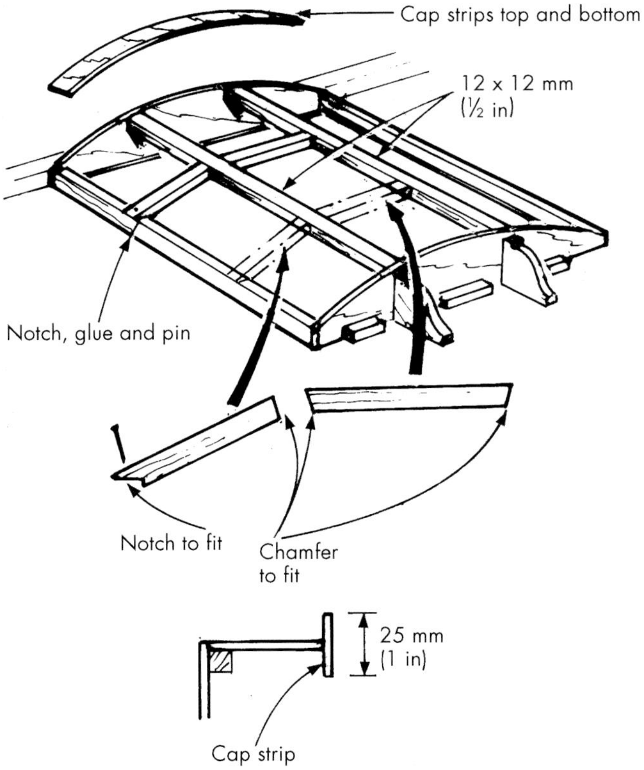

Cap strips top and bottom

12 x 12 mm (½ in)

Notch, glue and pin

Notch to fit

Chamfer to fit

25 mm (1 in)

Cap strip

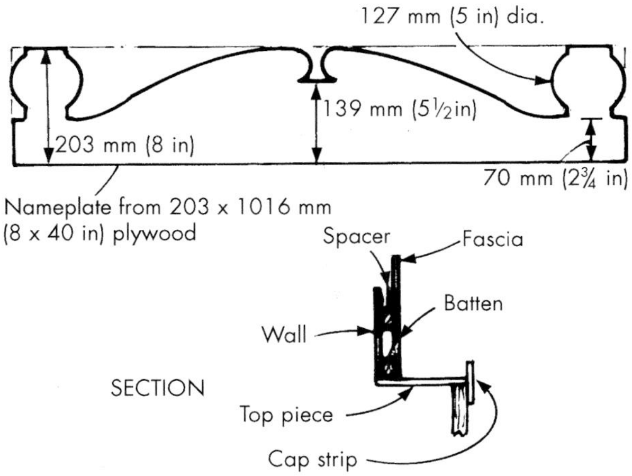

7 Make the shop nameplate to the shape shown in Fig. 7.8. It should come out of a plywood offcut. Always choose the narrowest offcut that will accommodate small pieces, so as to leave larger offcuts for the wider parts.

Smooth the edges and corners and glue and pin it to the top strips on the front wall. You may have to notch the curved edge strip over the window to clear it. There will be a space between the wall gable and the nameplate for the edge of the roof, which will be described later.

TIP: BAY WINDOW BARS

The bay window of the shop project has horizontal bars. These have to fit between the uprights. If you make one saw cut for each bar where it is to fit, you can turn the adjoining pieces over, as shown in the sketch. They will then fit against the opposite sides of the uprights which bisect the angle of the bay sides.

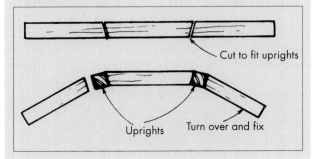

Cut to fit uprights

Uprights

Turn over and fix

8 The window in the side wall has a frame on the inside wall surface. This is easier to make than one that seats in the opening. Butt-join strips of 12 × 12 mm (½ in) pine as shown in Fig. 7.9.

Fig. 7.9

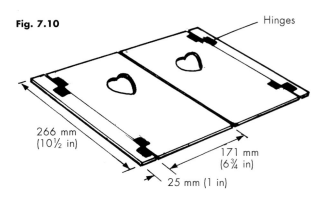

Glue frame flush with opening on inside face

All the vertical pieces fit between the top and bottom strips. Do not use panel pins when you glue the strips to the wall. Lay a strip of plywood under the central bar to keep it level, then put weights on the strips.

9 The shutters come next. Cut a pair, plus edge strips, to the pattern in Fig. 7.10, using up the piece of waste from the window itself, plus more small ply offcuts. Mark out the heart-shaped holes as shown in Fig. 7.11, then cut out with the jigsaw. Hinge the shutters to the edge strips with more webbing as already described, then glue the edge strips at the sides of the opening outside. You can add small catches or Velcro pads to hold them open or closed This completes work on the walls themselves. Bring the pairs of walls together at the joint corners and working from the outside, drill the joint strips for joining dowels, as described in Chapter 1.

Fig. 7.10

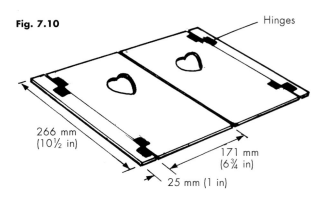

Hinges

266 mm (10½ in)

171 mm (6¾ in)

25 mm (1 in)

Fig. 7.11

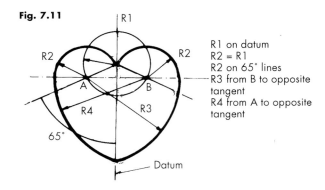

R1 on datum
R2 = R1
R2 on 65° lines
R3 from B to opposite tangent
R4 from A to opposite tangent

Datum

10 The roof panels that you cut earlier need hinging and edging. Arrange the hinges as shown in Fig. 7.12 and fix them as described earlier. Following Fig. 7.13, glue and pin 12 x 12 mm (½ in) strips under the front and back edges, clenching the pins over where they protrude through the strips before you continue.

Plane a 14 degree chamfer on the narrow edge of two strips of 12 × 18 mm (½ × ¾ in) pine. Glue and pin these under the side edges. Also glue two plywood gable pieces and a centre patch to the back edge of the roof. The pine strips at the front edge will hook over the front wall behind the nameplate, so you don't need gable pieces there.

Fig. 7.12

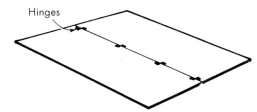

Hinges

Fig. 7.13

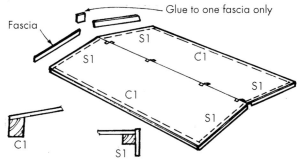

Glue to one fascia only

Fascia

S1
C1
S1
C1
S1
S1
C1
S1

11 The counter front has a recessed plinth. Make up the panel as shown in Fig. 7.14. Note that the back face is shown. The plinth sits on the bottom strip of 12 x 18 mm (½ × ¾ in) pine and the top strip supports the overhanging counter top. Cut the panel and plinth from the pieces of plywood offcut and turn the job outside face upwards, to fix the bottom and side rails. Then turn over as shown to clench the pins over, before you glue and pin the top rail on and the plinth strip to the bottom rail.

Fig. 7.14

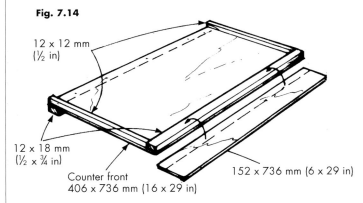

12 x 12 mm (½ in)

12 x 18 mm (½ × ¾ in)

Counter front
406 x 736 mm (16 x 29 in)

152 x 736 mm (6 x 29 in)

12 Make the two ends of the counter as shown in Fig. 7.15. After fixing the pine strips add a pair of 9 mm (⅜ in) dowels which will go

Fig. 7.15

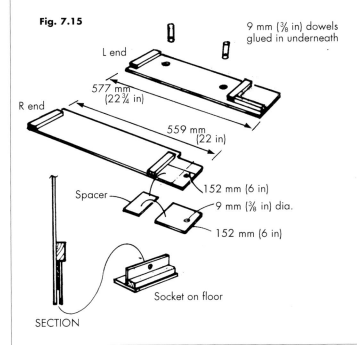

L end

9 mm (⅜ in) dowels glued in underneath

R end

577 mm (22 ¾ in)

559 mm (22 in)

Spacer

152 mm (6 in)

9 mm (⅜ in) dia.

152 mm (6 in)

Socket on floor

SECTION

through the side of the shop to steady and lock the end in place. The free end has a doubler and spacer below the lower strip. This fits over a locating piece, which you glue to the floor panel when you position the counter in the shop. Make this end panel shorter, as dimensioned in the figure, to allow for the thickness of the locating piece. Cut the counter top and flap from more plywood offcut and hinge them together as shown in Fig. 7.16. Glue and pin a strip of 12 × 12 mm (½ in) pine under the rear edge of the counter piece, before you fix the counter onto the top strips of the front and end panels. Make a storage shelf from plywood. Notch its corners to fit around the corner strips, then glue it onto the top edges of the bottom strips.

When you have assembled the walls loosely whilst standing inside, mark the position of the flap when it is horizontal. Glue a strip of 12 × 12 mm (½ in) pine there to support the flap when it is extended. The flap folds back onto the counter when open for access to the rear.

Fig. 7.16

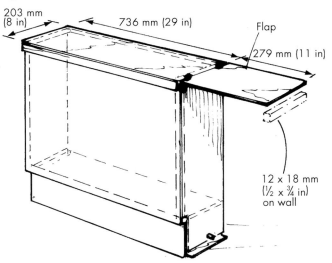

203 mm (8 in)

736 mm (29 in)

Flap

279 mm (11 in)

12 x 18 mm (½ × ¾ in) on wall

13 Space is limited at the back, so represent storage shelves by gluing narrow strips of Formica or other plastic laminate to the wall as spacers, then adding wider strips of plywood or hardboard. These will represent the edges of thick shelves – Fig. 7.17 shows this. The spacing strips are level with the bottom edges. This leaves a deep narrow groove, into which the owner can slide

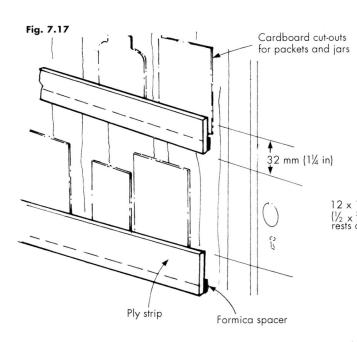

Fig. 7.17

Cardboard cut-outs for packets and jars

32 mm (1¼ in)

Ply strip

Formica spacer

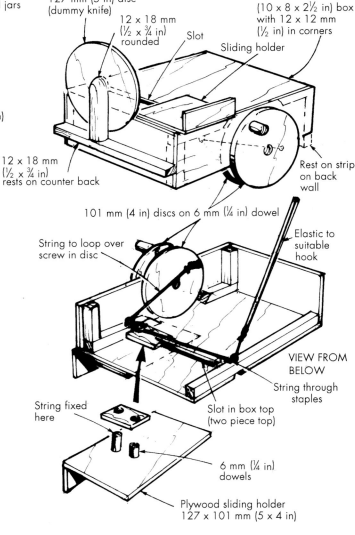

Fig. 7.18

127 mm (5 in) disc (dummy knife)

12 x 18 mm (½ x ¾ in) rounded

Slot

Sliding holder

254 x 203 x 63 mm (10 x 8 x 2½ in) box with 12 x 12 mm (½ x ½ in) in corners

12 x 18 mm (½ x ¾ in) rests on counter back

Rest on strip on back wall

101 mm (4 in) discs on 6 mm (¼ in) dowel

String to loop over screw in disc

Elastic to suitable hook

String fixed here

VIEW FROM BELOW

String through staples

Slot in box top (two piece top)

6 mm (¼ in) dowels

Plywood sliding holder 127 x 101 mm (5 x 4 in)

cardboard cut-outs of grocery items. The children can make these by cutting pieces of card with brand names upon them from used packets, and sticking paper labels from tins onto the back of other cereal packet card. Cut the edges to shape, to represent bottles, packets and cans.

14 Drill holes in the walls and, using pliers, bend some hooks from coat-hanger wire. Double all ends back to avoid sharp ends. These hooks can be used to hang up items for display, such as clothes on hangers, coils of rope, seaside buckets, and spades. Glue wooden spring-type clothes pegs there too, for gripping magazines and light items. Have a collection of strong cardboard boxes glued together to form bins for junk, books and vegetables. These can go under the bay window inside and outside.

15 A kitchen scale or balance and a toy cash register can go on the counter, and if you feel like a spot of mechanical modelling, add the old-fashioned bacon slicer shown in Fig. 7.18. It is really quite simple to make: a cord on a crank pulls the bacon table forward and a rubber band returns it. Rub a pencil all over the dowels that form the guide rails, for smooth action.

16 Sand all sharp edges and corners, fill over hollows and where clenching has been done. Also fill and level any areas of open grain and any small gaps.

Paint the inside in light colours, but introduce darker areas where older items are displayed. Make the counter front appear panelled, by use of different wood colour varnish stains and ruled panel lines in light and dark paint, in the manner of stage scenery.

The style of the shop outside looks best if traditional materials such as stone and brick are represented. Children's imagination spans a greater time range than the immediate present.

Future Home

Do you want a contrast? How about going to year 2010, where one may live in a more compact, environmentally friendly and energy efficient habitat. Let the children grow to realise that fuel energy can be conserved by the insulation of a lawn over the roof, and part of the home recessed into a bank. Windows can incorporate solar panels and a garden pool becomes a fish tank to admit a little more light. The compact work and entertainment unit is flexible, and furnishing too is multi-purpose; even the front door becomes an outdoor picnic table. Domestic droid and pet, who are part of the scene, would consume no food.

 The home has a floor area of 1016 mm (40 in) square and a maximum headroom of 1117 mm (44 in). Construction is similar to the previous projects, although plywood with a thicker centre lamination would be an advantage.

STAR RATING
Skill level ***
Cost ****
Child height ****

MATERIALS

6 mm (¼ in) plywood (equal rigidity): 12 sheets 2438 × 1219 mm (8 × 4 ft)	25 mm (1 in) strong upholstery webbing 2083 mm (82 in)
4 mm (³⁄₁₆ in) plywood: 1 sheet 2438 × 1219 mm (8 × 4 ft)	4 small castors
Offcuts of 3 mm (⅛ in) plywood	2 mm (³⁄₃₂ in) clear styrene glazing: 533 × 482 mm (21 × 19 in)
15 × 63 mm (⅝ × 2½ in) pine: 2 at 1981 mm (78 in)	Imitation grass matting: 838 × 1041 mm (33 × 41 in)
9 × 76 mm (⅜ × 3 in) pine: 940 mm (37 in) cut from cladding strip	2 pairs 25 mm (1 in) hinges and screws
9 × 51 mm (⅜ × 2 in) pine: 2 at 711 mm (28 in) cut from cladding strip	2 at 18 mm (¾ in) no. 10 roundhead woodscrews
18 × 44 mm (¾ × 1¾ in) pine: 406 mm (16 in)	20 mm (¾ in) panel pins
	Thin card
12 × 18 mm (½ × ¾ in) pine: 4 at 1066 mm (42 in)	'Invisible' nylon sewing thread
8 at 1016 mm (40 in)	2 table-tennis balls
2 at 914 mm (36 in)	Fur fabric: 0.5 m (½ yd)
4 at 762 mm (30 in)	Waste expanded poly-styrene packing
12 × 12 mm (½ in) pine: 2 at 1600 mm (63 in)	Small foam cushion(s)
	Velcro
9 mm (⅜ in) hardwood dowel: 152 mm (6 in)	Coat-hanger wire
	Spring clothes peg
6 mm (¼ in) hardwood dowel: 762 mm (30 in)	PVA glue
	Glue sticks
	Abrasive paper
	Decorator's filler
	Non-toxic paint

TOOLS

• Hand saw or hand-held circular saw	• Hot-melt glue gun
• Tenon saw	• Domestic iron
• Jigsaw	• Scissors
• Chisel	• Stanley knife
• Hammer	• Sanding block
• Nail punch	• Pencil
• Screwdriver	• Compass
• Drill	• Rule
• Pliers	• Try square/sliding bevel
	• Paint brushes

Fig. 8.1

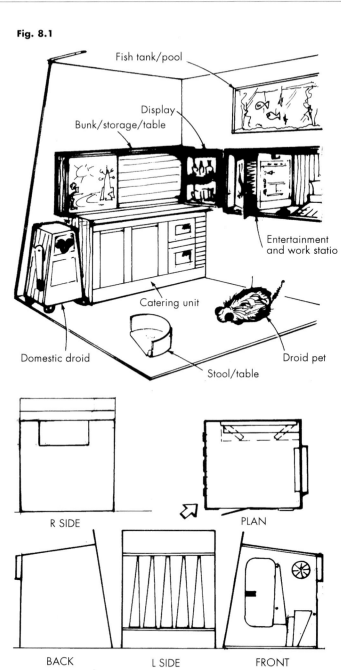

Fish tank/pool
Display
Bunk/storage/table
Entertainment and work statio
Catering unit
Droid pet
Domestic droid
Stool/table

R SIDE   PLAN

BACK   L SIDE   FRONT

1 Mark out the three sheets of plywood according to Fig. 8.2. Note the different thicknesses
required to provide the strength where needed.
Cut the panels from one sheet at a time and keep
them flat until the next stage of work. You can use
a hand-held circular saw for speed, setting the
depth to cut shallow, so that the edge is less likely
to be rough. Lay a thick piece of timber under the

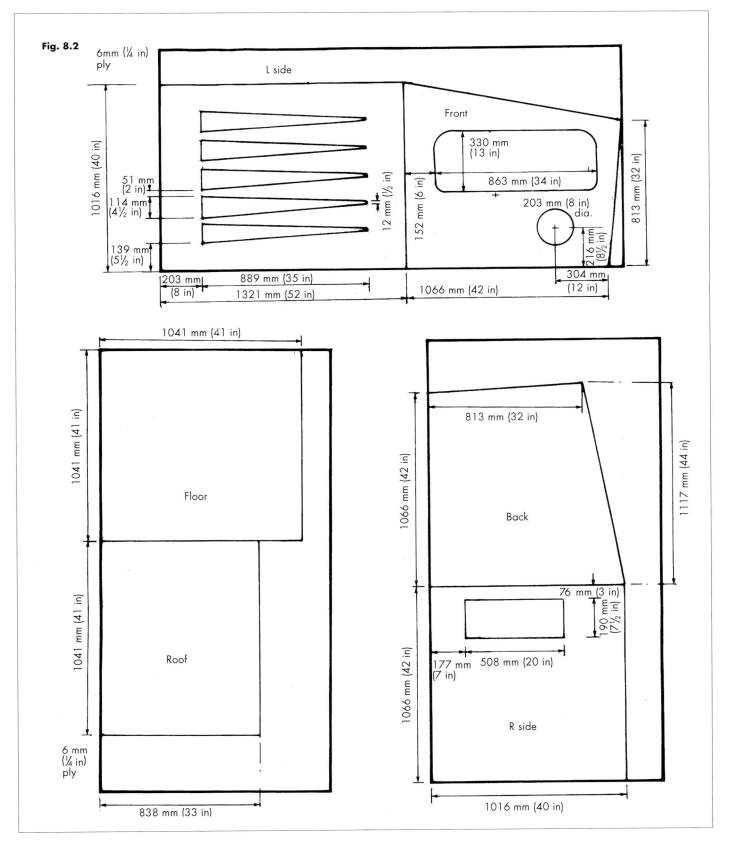

plywood, near the cutting line and work on the floor. If the job is supported on a portable work-bench it will tend to bend, whereas the floor will support slightly drooping narrow pieces as they are parted off.

Fig. 8.3

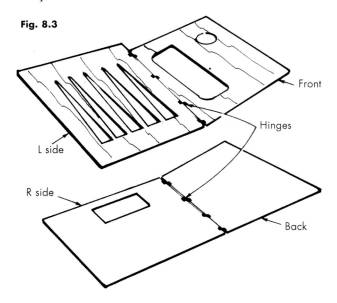

Fig. 8.4

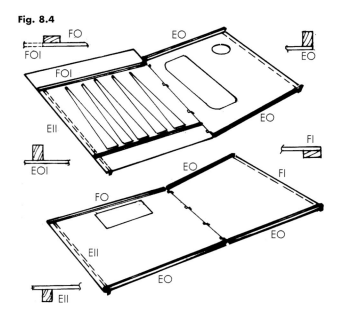

Fig. 8.5

254 x 533 mm (10 x 21 in)

6mm (¼ in) dowel

12 x 12 mm (½ in) inside

9 x 76 mm (⅜ x 3 in) frame (from cladding strip) size O.A. 254 x 533 mm (10 x 21 in)

Styrene glazing over hole in wall, fix with glue gun

R wall

2 Hinge together the two pairs of wall panels as shown in Fig. 8.3. Lay them flat on the floor while doing this, to ensure that the edges are aligned. Use hot-melt glue to fix the eight pairs of webbing strips, which should each be 38 mm (1½ in) long. The hinging technique is explained in Chapter 1. Finish off with the domestic iron, as described. You may have noticed that the doors also are hinged at this stage on other projects. This comes later here.

3 With the panels outer face upwards, as in Fig. 8.4, glue and pin the 12 × 18 mm (½ × ¾ in) reinforcement strips under the edges, starting with the one that is laid flat, then those which are on edge. Turn the panels over and com-plete the job, again starting with the flat-placed strip, then the three others, on each pair of panels.

4 The opening in the left wall is a fish tank/gar-den pond panel. Follow Fig. 8.5, making the box frame from 9 × 76 mm (⅜ × 3 in) pine butt-joined with glue and panel pins. Cut a shallow notch in each top end to take a 6 mm (¼ in) dowel which will be used for suspending a fish mobile.

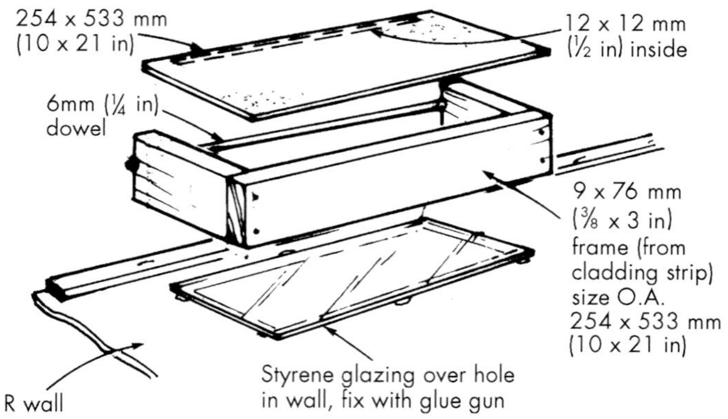

Glue the dowel in place. Cut a panel for the back as shown, glue a strip of 12 × 12 mm (½ in) pine inside the top edge, then glue and pin it over the frame and paint the inside faces of the box a muddy green. Lay some green strips of paper and lichen against the side strips to represent water plants, and sprinkle sand or grit on the bottom. All this is necessary to avoid splashing the glazing, which you now cut with a fine-tooth saw, or score with a Stanley knife equipped with a laminate-cutting blade.

Secure the glazing to the outside of the wall with dabs of hot-melt glue at the edges. Then fix the box to the wall around it with PVA glue. Put weights on it while the wall is flat on the floor.

Fig. 8.6

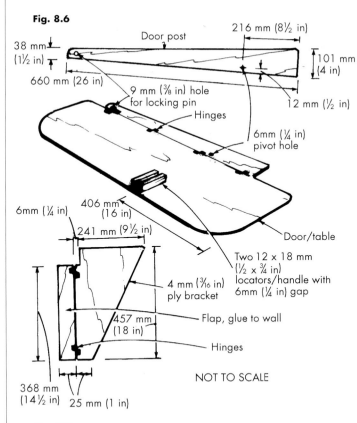

Door post

38 mm (1½ in)

660 mm (26 in)

216 mm (8½ in)

101 mm (4 in)

12 mm (½ in)

9 mm (⅜ in) hole for locking pin

Hinges

6mm (¼ in) pivot hole

6mm (¼ in)

406 mm (16 in)

241 mm (9½ in)

4 mm (³⁄₁₆ in) ply bracket

457 mm (18 in)

Door/table

Two 12 x 18 mm (½ x ¾ in) locators/handle with 6mm (¼ in) gap

Flap, glue to wall

Hinges

NOT TO SCALE

368 mm (14½ in)

25 mm (1 in)

Fig. 8.7

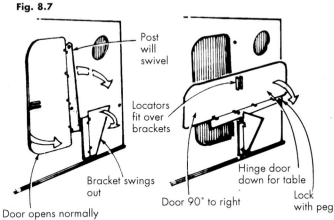

Post will swivel

Locators fit over brackets

Bracket swings out

Door opens normally

Door 90° to right

Hinge door down for table

Lock with peg

5 The entry door is hinged to a swinging support which pivots at the side of the opening. Follow the dimensions and assembly in Fig. 8.6. An offcut from the tapered window slits in the left wall will provide the material for the support.

Also make the hinged bracket that will open out from the wall below the door and engage with the strip wood handle. Check the dimensions as you

work, so that when the door is pivoted it forms a table as shown in the sequence in Fig. 8.7. Glue a small piece of 12 × 18 mm (½ × ¾ in) pine behind the pivot position to give the pivot screw extra purchase. You can use a small piece of Velcro to hold the bracket tidily against the wall in its folded position.

6 On the inside of the left wall there is a box unit representing an audio/visual unit and work station (Fig. 8.8). In order that the walls may fold together for storage, this piece will hang from hooks. Start by making the box frame from 9 × 51 mm (⅜ × 2 in) pine. Cut notches in the top and bottom strips as shown, to take the ends of sliding and rotating pieces of 6 mm (¼ in) dowel. Glue and pin the corners of the box, then cut a piece of thin plywood offcut (or hardboard) for the back. Tack it loosely on the back while you make the other components.

Fig. 8.8

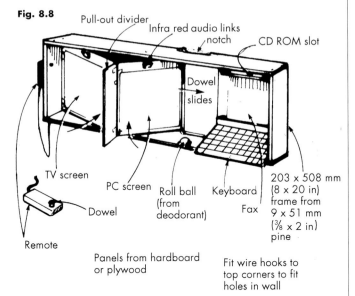

Pull-out divider

Infra red audio links

notch

CD ROM slot

Dowel slides

TV screen

PC screen

Roll ball (from deodorant)

Keyboard

Fax

Dowel

Remote

Panels from hardboard or plywood

203 x 508 mm (8 x 20 in) frame from 9 x 51 mm (⅜ x 2 in) pine

Fit wire hooks to top corners to fit holes in wall

Cut the two screen pieces and a divider from thin plywood to fit loosely between top and bottom, then make and fit the dummy keyboard and fax compartment from thin strip wood and plywood offcuts, as shown in the illustration. The exact sizes are not important, so long as you leave space for the two screens to lie flat against the back panel. Now hinge the screens together in the centre, slip two pieces of webbing between the joint and glue it to the divider and back of one of

Fig. 8.9

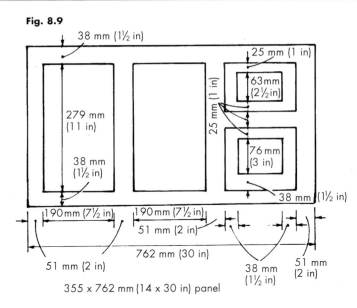

355 x 762 mm (14 x 30 in) panel

the screens. Glue a dowel to the outer edge of each screen.

Remove the back and drop the dowels into the notches, before gluing and pinning the back on. The screens should now hinge from the left dowel and the right dowel, which slides in its long notch. Bend a pair of hooks from coat-hanger wire and secure one to each top corner with hot-melt glue and a webbing patch. Make corresponding holes in the wall under the pool display.

7 The largest item is a domestic station: freezer, cooker, and combined wash and waste unit. Following Fig. 8.9, mark out the front panel on the largest plywood offcut and cut out the doors and glazing holes. Hinge the door as shown in Fig. 8.10. Glue and pin a strip of 12 × 18 mm (½ × ¾ in) pine flat at the top edge. Make the shelf, ends, and dividers, from narrow offcuts of plywood and glue and pin strips of 12 × 12 mm (½ in) pine where shown in Fig. 8.11. These will provide gluing area when you assemble the unit. Clench any panel pins over before assembly, or they may

Fig. 8.10

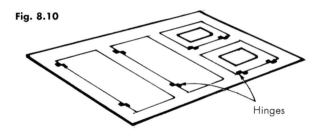

Hinges

Fig. 8.11

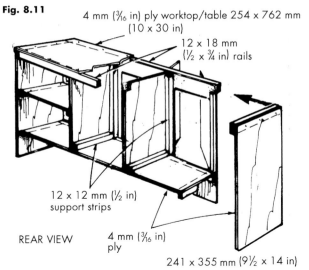

4 mm (³⁄₁₆ in) ply worktop/table 254 x 762 mm (10 x 30 in)

12 x 18 mm (½ x ¾ in) rails

12 x 12 mm (½ in) support strips

REAR VIEW

4 mm (³⁄₁₆ in) ply

241 x 355 mm (9½ x 14 in)

be inaccessible after doing so. There should be a notch at the top rear corner of the dividers, to clear the 12 × 18 mm (½ × ¾ in) strip. Glue and pin the latter on edge under the top panel, which you then glue and pin to the top strips at front and ends. This surface becomes a table or preparation area.

When painted, glaze the oven doors from behind, using the remainder of the styrene sheet, secured with dabs of hot-melt glue.

8 Resting on the table will be a bunk, which will lean against the wall to reveal two storage racks. These swing out to support it and provide space for dishes and dry goods. Fig. 8.12 shows the construction and sizes. It can also be used on the floor, as a low seat. When closed, the racks retain their (unspillable) contents.

Fig. 8.12

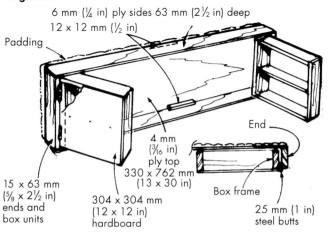

6 mm (¼ in) ply sides 63 mm (2½ in) deep

12 x 12 mm (½ in)

Padding

End

4 mm (³⁄₁₆ in) ply top 330 x 762 mm (13 x 30 in)

15 x 63 mm (⅝ x 2½ in) ends and box units

304 x 304 mm (12 x 12 in) hardboard

Box frame

25 mm (1 in) steel butts

Fig. 8.13

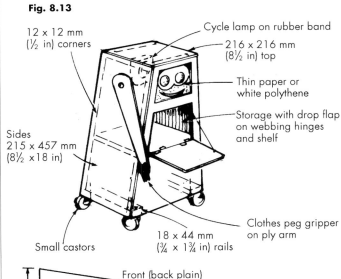

12 x 12 mm (½ in) corners

Cycle lamp on rubber band

216 x 216 mm (8½ in) top

Thin paper or white polythene

Storage with drop flap on webbing hinges and shelf

Sides 215 x 457 mm (8½ x 18 in)

Clothes peg gripper on ply arm

Small castors

18 x 44 mm (¾ x 1¾ in) rails

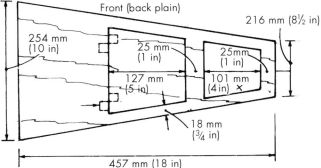

Front (back plain)

216 mm (8½ in)

254 mm (10 in)

25 mm (1 in)

25mm (1 in)

127 mm (5 in)

101 mm (4 in) ×

18 mm (¾ in)

457 mm (18 in)

9 Friendly, if not truly robotic, the domestic droid shown in Fig. 8.13 should provide service as a transport trolley and carrier of small items in its clothes-peg claw. It can be pulled along on a string. Construction is similar to that of the domestic station in stage 7. A strip of 18 × 44 mm

(¾ × 1¾ in) pine supports each pair of small castors. Chamfer the outer edge of these strips to match the slope of the sides. Hang a cycle lamp inside the top to shine through a paper or white polythene screen (face). This will cause an area of light to move about as the lamp swings around when the droid is pulled.

10 An appropriate pet might be a furry little android, based on a radio controlled toy car or buggy. Make this light in weight, to suit the vehicle borrowed for the occasion – see Fig. 8.14.

Measure the shape it has to enclose, then form a cardboard box to fit, carve waste expanded polystyrene to a half-pear shape, and hollow it to fit over the box. The rest is up to the sewing department, to make a long-haired fur fabric 'skin' and add table tennis ball eyes on pieces of elastic, so that they roll when the buggy jerks about.

Fig. 8.15

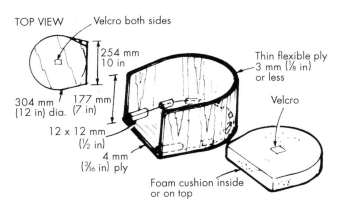

TOP VIEW

Velcro both sides

254 mm 10 in

Thin flexible ply 3 mm (⅛ in) or less

Velcro

304 mm (12 in) dia.

177 mm (7 in)

12 x 12 mm (½ in)

4 mm (³⁄₁₆ in) ply

Foam cushion inside or on top

11 One or two small adaptable chairs will complete the scene. You need a small cushion for each. Fig. 8.15 shows the thin plywood construction. They can be laid upside down on the floor with cushion inside as tub chairs, upright as small tables, or as padded stools with the cushion on top.

12 Use colour coordinated schemes, so as to give an uncluttered appearance inside the play-house. Fix imitation grass mat to the roof area and cut out some small fish shapes from thin card. Paint them bright colours. Suspend them singly and in pairs on 'invisible' nylon thread from the dowel in the 'pond'.

Fig. 8.14

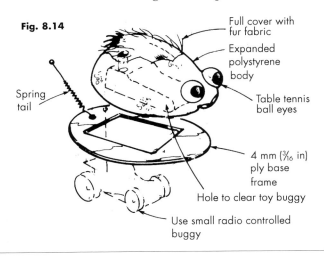

Full cover with fur fabric

Expanded polystyrene body

Table tennis ball eyes

Spring tail

4 mm (³⁄₁₆ in) ply base frame

Hole to clear toy buggy

Use small radio controlled buggy

Camper

There is more than an accommodating space for domestic play here. This camper van caters for the pretend driver as well. It is a compact, vehicle-styled, play-house in which the driving seat converts to become part of a living, sleeping and cooking unit, and a removable awning extends the play area when the 'destination' is reached.

It is not important that the wheels do not make it actually mobile. How many times have you seen children seated in a packing case or upturned table which serves as a bus or a ship? This project has a steering wheel, gear lever and indicator controls, folding table, bunk seats for little ones or dolls, a sink, and a cooker with controls that give gas flame effects.

While the driver has a raised cab floor with seated headroom of 813 mm (32 in), the floor of the accommodation area is actually on the ground or room floor. This gives standing headroom of 1066 mm (42 in). In stepping over the door threshold, rather than up onto it, 152 mm (6 in) of height is gained without making the proportions too tall and unconvincing. From the outside, the lower part with wheel arches is inset to give the effect that the van floor is above ground level. Inside, this is disguised by the seating.

The project occupies a floor area of 1092 × 762 mm (43 × 30 in) (plus 813 mm (32 in) for the awning) and folds up to a package 1092 × 203 mm (43 × 8 in) against a wall, with the small components stacked on top.

STAR RATING
Skill ****
Cost **
Child height ****

MATERIALS

4 mm (³⁄₁₆ in) plywood:
  2 sheets 2438 ×
  1219 mm (8 × 4 ft)
  1 half sheet 1219 ×
  1219 mm (4 × 4 ft)
44 × 32 mm (1¾ × 1¼ in)
  pine: 51 mm (2 in)
12 × 18 mm (½ × ¾ in)
  pine: 4 at 1066 mm
  (42 in)
  10 at 762 mm (30 in)
  4 at 711 mm (28 in)
  4 at 406 mm (16 in)
12 × 12 mm (½ in) pine:
  2 at 1168 mm (46 in)
  2 at 660 mm (26 in)
9 mm (³⁄₈ in) dowel: 2 at
  1219 mm (48 in)
  1 at 406 mm (16 in)

25 mm (1 in)-wide strong
  upholstery webbing:
  1676 mm (66 in)
Curtain spring: 203 mm
  (8 in)
9 mm (³⁄₈ in) rubber or soft
  plastic tube: 76 mm (3 in)
Striped light fabric: 1 m
  (1 yd)
3 at 25 mm (1 in) no. 8
  roundhead woodscrews
Sewing thread
PVA glue
Glue sticks
Panel pins
Filler
Abrasive paper
Non-toxic paint

TOOLS

- Hand saw or hand-held circular saw
- Tenon saw
- Hand-held jigsaw
- Plane
- Hammer
- Nail punch
- Drill
- Screwdriver
- Glue gun
- Domestic iron
- Scissors
- G-cramps
- Sanding block or sander
- Pencil
- Rule
- Try square
- Filling knife
- Paint brushes

Fig. 9.1

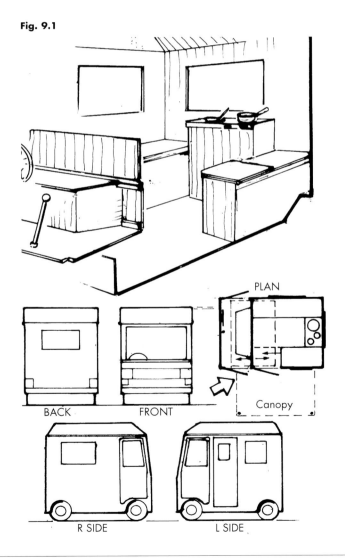

PLAN

BACK   FRONT   Canopy

R SIDE   L SIDE

1 All the plywood components just fit onto two and a half sheets of plywood. Fig. 9.2 shows how to mark them out. Many parts share the same cutting line, so you save time. Take care, however, that you do not veer off the lines when you are cutting, or one part may lose some width. The dimensions allow for the thickness of the saw cut (or kerf). Where there are doors, this gives the necessary clearance. The lower part of each side panel will slide up slightly to form wheel arches and a dummy sill. This is why the 'wheel' radiuses are separated slightly for marking out. The bottom line is straight and the wheels painted on. Stack the pieces on a flat surface until you need them, otherwise they may warp.

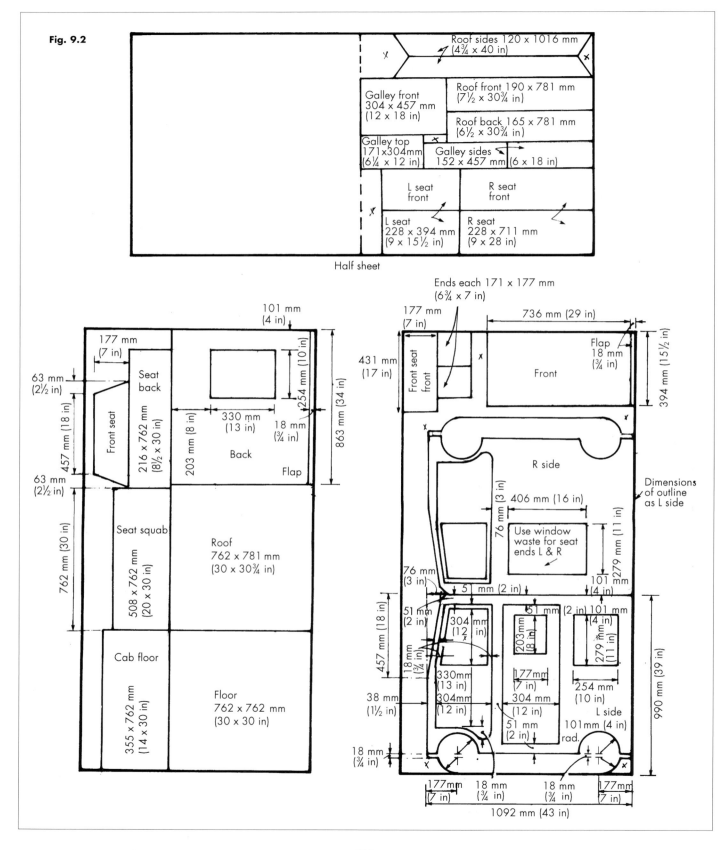

Fig. 9.2

Roof sides 120 x 1016 mm (4¾ x 40 in)

Galley front 304 x 457 mm (12 x 18 in)

Roof front 190 x 781 mm (7½ x 30¾ in)

Roof back 165 x 781 mm (6½ x 30¾ in)

Galley top 171 x 304 mm (6¼ x 12 in)

Galley sides 152 x 457 mm (6 x 18 in)

L seat front

R seat front

L seat 228 x 394 mm (9 x 15½ in)

R seat 228 x 711 mm (9 x 28 in)

Half sheet

101 mm (4 in)

177 mm (7 in)

63 mm (2½ in)

457 mm (18 in)

63 mm (2½ in)

762 mm (30 in)

Seat back

Front seat

Seat squab 508 x 762 mm (20 x 30 in)

Cab floor 355 x 762 mm (14 x 30 in)

216 x 762 mm (8½ x 30 in)

203 mm (8 in)

330 mm (13 in)

Back

Roof 762 x 781 mm (30 x 30¾ in)

Floor 762 x 762 mm (30 x 30 in)

254 mm (10 in)

863 mm (34 in)

18 mm (¾ in)

Flap

Ends each 171 x 177 mm (6¾ x 7 in)

177 mm (7 in)

736 mm (29 in)

431 mm (17 in)

Front seat front

Front

Flap 18 mm (¾ in)

394 mm (15½ in)

R side

406 mm (16 in)

76 mm (3 in)

Use window waste for seat ends L & R

279 mm (11 in)

101 mm (4 in)

Dimensions of outline as L side

76 mm (3 in)

457 mm (18 in)

51 mm (2 in)

18 mm (¾ in)

5 mm (2 in)

304 mm (12 in)

330 mm (13 in)

304 mm (12 in)

51 mm (2 in)

203 mm (8 in)

177 mm (7 in)

304 mm (12 in)

51 mm (2 in)

101 mm (4 in)

279 mm (11 in)

254 mm (10 in)

L side

101 mm (4 in) rad.

990 mm (39 in)

38 mm (1½ in)

18 mm (¾ in)

177 mm (7 in)

18 mm (¾ in)

18 mm (¾ in)

177 mm (7 in)

1092 mm (43 in)

2 The front panel needs a hinged edge flap, so that when folded up, it clears the inset side part. Fig. 9.3 shows the positions of the webbing hinges, which you fix according to the sequence in Chapter 1. That edge flap will be fixed to the side panel, rather than there being a hinge line actually on the corner.

The same applies to the other side and back panel assembly, shown in Fig. 9.4.

Fig. 9.3

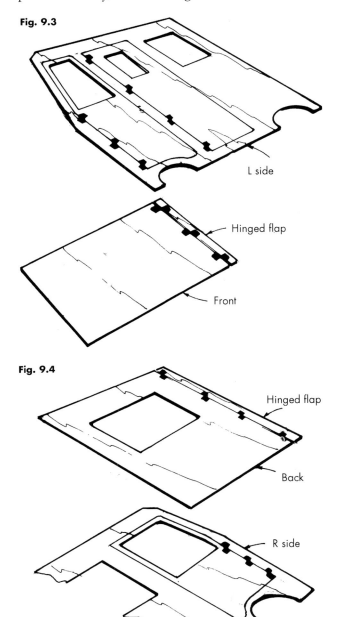

L side

Hinged flap

Front

Fig. 9.4

Hinged flap

Back

R side

3 Before fitting the front and back panels, cut pieces of 12 × 18 mm (½ × ¾ in) pine. Glue and pin them, laid flat to form a staggered joint between the lower and main parts of the side panels. Fig. 9.5 shows the left side detail. Repeat this, opposite-handed, for the right side.

Fig. 9.5

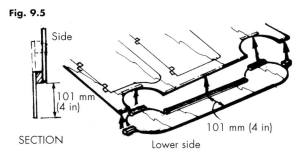

Side

101 mm (4 in)

SECTION

101 mm (4 in)

Lower side

4 Glue and pin strips of 12 × 18 mm (½ × ¾ in) pine to the left side and front panel as in Fig. 9.6. Note which are on edge, and which are laid flat, inside or outside. The small details around this diagram show the relative placement. There are no strips on the narrow hinged flaps.

Fig. 9.6

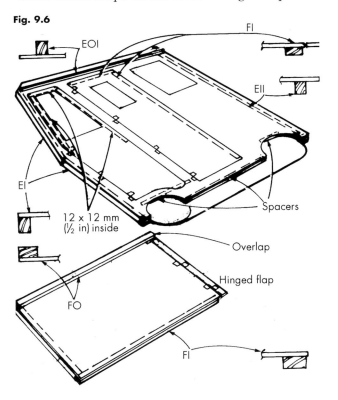

EOl

Fl

Ell

El

Spacers

12 × 12 mm (½ in) inside

FO

Overlap

Hinged flap

Fl

75

5 Fig. 9.7 shows the back panel with edging strips fixed in the same way. Note that the bottom strip extends over, but is not glued to, the hinged flap.

When the glue has set, plane the top of the panel and the corner of the top strip to a 45 degree chamfer, so that the roof box fits over it.

Fig. 9.7

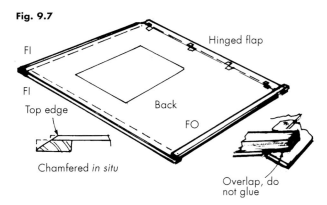

FI

FI

Top edge

Chamfered *in situ*

Hinged flap

Back

FO

Overlap, do not glue

6 The strips that reinforce the upper parts of the driver and passenger doors extend down past the window openings, as shown in Fig. 9.8. Note the butt joints at the top and the chamfer on the front to follow the edge of the door.

Fig. 9.8

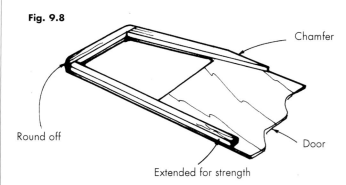

Chamfer

Round off

Extended for strength

Door

7 When you fix the edge strips on the right-hand side panel, note from Fig. 9.9 that the lower piece is inset for a quick-detach joint and the upper part is flush, like the left-hand one.

8 Now join the back and front assemblies to their appropriate sides. Fig. 9.10 shows how the front edge flap is glued and pinned to the flush side strip, and Fig. 9.11 shows the back flap going

Fig. 9.9

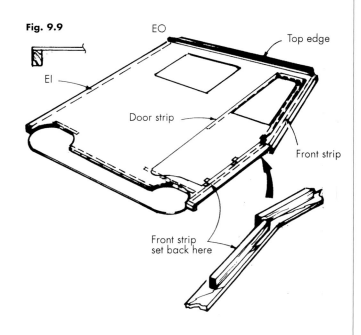

EO

Top edge

EI

Door strip

Front strip

Front strip set back here

Fig. 9.10

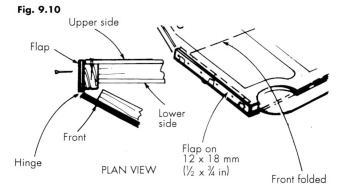

Upper side

Flap

Front

Hinge

PLAN VIEW

Lower side

Flap on 12 x 18 mm (½ x ¾ in)

Front folded

Fig. 9.11

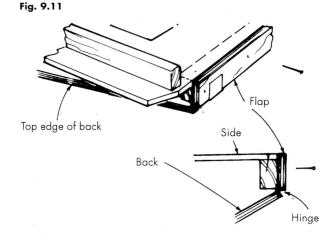

Top edge of back

Flap

Side

Back

Hinge

onto the right rear side strip. To be workmanlike about it, shave a fraction off the strips where the hinges are to meet them. Pin close to the hinge positions to ensure a good glue bond, and clench all points over when the job is opened out again. Drill the joiner strips and fit the 9mm (⅜ in) quick-detach dowels, as shown in Chapter 1.

9 The roof is a shaped box that will sit on the top strips on each side panel. Cut all the components from plywood and glue and pin strips of 12 × 12 mm (½ in) to the side pieces, as shown in Fig. 9.12. Chamfer the meeting ends and clench the panel pin points over.

While the glue sets, plane the narrow edge of a piece of 12 × 18 mm (½ × ¾ in) pine to 45 degrees. It is to fit between the assembled sides of the windscreen, so each end will be inset. Glue and pin it to the front edge of the angled front panel. The latter is at a shallower angle, so the strip matches the slope of the windscreen. Plane and sand the top edges of the front and rear panels to sit under the top panel.

Support the edge strips of the sides and using plenty of PVA glue, fix the top in position. Put

more panel pins into the edge strips and turn the assembly upside down on a flat surface. Do not pin the top to end joints. Mix sawdust with more PVA glue and form a fillet on the inside of these two joints. Leave the job flat until set, then clench the pin points over. When thoroughly set, plane and sand all the top edges and corners to a rounded shape, as shown in Fig. 9.13.

Fig. 9.13

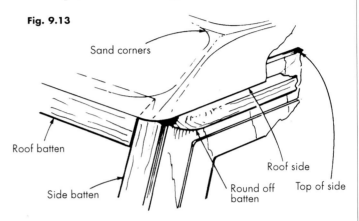

10 Cut the main floor panel and glue a narrow offcut vertically at the front edge to hide the front wheels from inside. The cutaway sketch in Fig. 9.14 shows this and the corner strip of 12 × 12 mm (½ in) pine.

Fig. 9.14

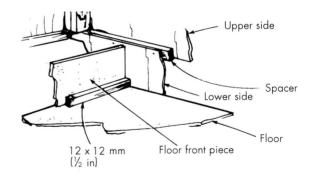

Fig. 9.12

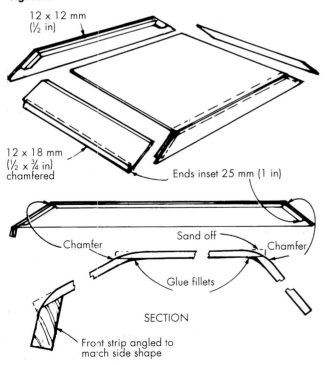

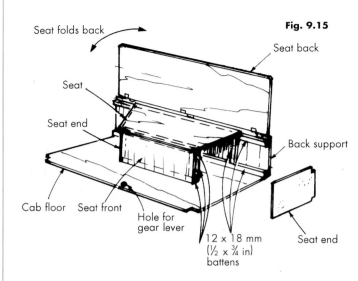

Fig. 9.15

Seat folds back

Seat back

Seat

Seat end

Back support

Cab floor   Seat front

Hole for
gear lever

Seat end

12 x 18 mm
(½ x ¾ in)
battens

11 The cab interior is a drop-in assembly, with a floor notched to fit around the front corner strips and rest on the spacer strips each side. Fig. 9.15 shows the construction and dimensions.

Hinge the folding seat back to the upright rear panel, then glue and pin the corner strips to the front and rear upright panels. Next, fix the seat ends to them to hold them square. When set, glue and pin the seat on top. Sand the corners of the seat and those on the strips each side, then drill a hole near the front of the floor to take the gear lever.

12 Make the gear lever from dowel, as in Fig. 9.16, and add a wooden ball or table tennis ball to the top. Glue into a scrap of flexible tube and insert this into the hole in the floor.

The same sketch also shows the steering wheel and indicator controls, with the important dimensions. Sand the wheel well for comfortable

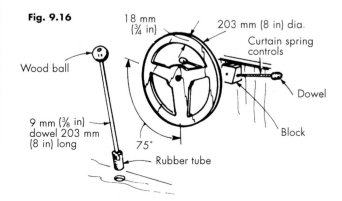

Fig. 9.16

18 mm
(¾ in)

203 mm (8 in) dia.

Curtain spring
controls

Wood ball

Dowel

9 mm (⅜ in)
dowel 203 mm
(8 in) long

75°

Block

Rubber tube

handling and chamfer that small piece of 44 × 32 mm (1¾ × 1¼ in) pine to form a mounting block, drilled for the wheel pivot screw and for two pieces of curtain spring that make flexible minor controls with dowel scraps in the ends. Glue the block to the front panel near the top edge (left- or right-handed, depending on which side one wishes to drive).

13 Make both seats for the rear compartment in a similar way. They are shown in Fig. 9.17. Hinge the flap on the left-hand seat before adding the corner and back strips. Each seat rests on the floor panel and leans against the side. Their back strips sit on the spacer strips and the flap rests on the folded edge of the driver's seat when it is in the table or bunk position. When the caravan door is open it forms a service hatch shelf to the outside picnic area.

Fig. 9.17

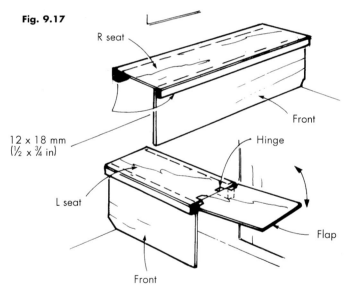

R seat

Front

12 x 18 mm
(½ x ¾ in)

Hinge

L seat

Flap

Front

14 The galley unit has a tub sink (empty plastic container). There is a flame effect on the dummy gas burners. Start by marking out and cutting the top as shown in Fig. 9.18 (which is one quarter actual size). A template for the flame-effect cut-outs is provided at the lower part of the same figure. Make the two shutters, shown dotted, and pivot them temporarily on 25 mm (1 in) screws, as shown.

Fig. 9.18

¼ FULL SIZE

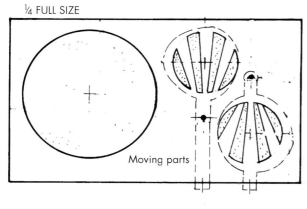

Moving parts

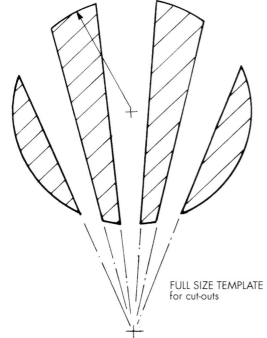

FULL SIZE TEMPLATE
for cut-outs

Fig. 9.19

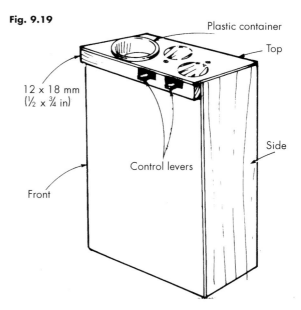

Plastic container

Top

12 x 18 mm
(½ x ¾ in)

Side

Control levers

Front

Move both levers to the right and mark through the slits in the top. Remove the shutters and glue a small piece of wood under the screw hole in each. Paint the marked areas light blue to represent gas flames, then paint the rest black. Paint black circles on the top at each burner position, including the cut edges of the slots. Re-mount the shutters on their screws. When they are moved left, the whole area will appear black, for the 'off' position. When moved to the right, the blue will show to represent fully 'on'.

15 Cut the front and side panels and add 12 × 12 mm (½ in) pine corner strips at the front and top edges of the latter. Glue and pin a top strip to the front, then notch it to clear the 'gas' levers, limiting each of their movements to the correct amount for best effect. When this has been done to your satisfaction, glue and pin the top in place and the front to the sides via the corner strips. Fix the empty plastic tub with hot-melt glue into the hole you cut to fit it. The prototype has a used putty tub, but ice cream or butter tubs may fit. Collect this before you start!

The finished galley stands on the floor panel against the back, with a seat each side – see Fig. 9.19.

16 With first one side, then the other hinged open for access, check that the seats and cab floor seat firmly on the side spacers and rails. If you find that they are not secure, form lips on these with narrow plywood strips, to hook under the edge strips of the seats. The rear of the driver's floor should also sit on the front panel that you fixed to the main floor. When you have drilled and fitted the quick-detach dowels at the front and rear corners, as shown in the other projects, the assembly will be more rigid. The roof box will keep it square.

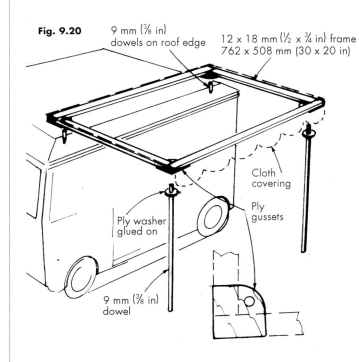

Fig. 9.20

9 mm (⅜ in) dowels on roof edge

12 × 18 mm (½ × ¾ in) frame 762 × 508 mm (30 × 20 in)

Cloth covering

Ply gussets

Ply washer glued on

9 mm (⅜ in) dowel

9 mm (⅜ in) dowel. Form flats on the side of two short pieces of dowel and glue them securely to the roof box side to engage in the gussets.

Make two plywood washers and glue them as shown near the top ends of a pair of 1219 mm (48 in) lengths of dowel, which form the awning posts. Cover the frame with fabric, which should have a scalloped edge to hang down as shown. Stretch the fabric and staple it in place all round the edges. The awning and posts can be carried on the top of the roof when 'driving'.

18 Check that all folding panels clear the sides when moved – trim if necessary. Sand and fill to remove sharp edges, corners and hollows. Paint the inside and outside light colours. All the windows and windscreen are left unglazed and have no frames such as are shown on other projects. The camper can be made to look longer when you add a horizontal stripe in contrasting colour, a lower band of a different tone, and dark grey roof and under the sills. Paint the tyres black and spray the hubs silver, using a paper stencil. Add details like headlamps, indicators and rear clusters, in paint and metallic adhesive tape. This can also be used to represent the bumpers. Finish with number plates that include the owner's initials.

17 Make up a frame from 12 × 18 mm (½ × ¾ in) strip and plywood corner gussets, as shown in Fig. 9.20. Drill each gusset for a free fit in

Space Capsule

If you need a play-house that is *really* compact, make this capsule. It affords the atmosphere of a shuttle or space probe and one, two or even three young astronauts can sit, squat or curl up inside to operate the dummy controls, rest, and kneel or stand to direct a 'cherry-picker' arm. There is a star monitor screen, which shows changing positions of 'stars' and a meteorite deflector that gives thumps to the outside surface. It is entered by a crawl-through hatch and is lit via eight ports in the nose cone.

You can see from Figs. 10.1 and 10.2 that the capsule is octagonal in plan form. It measures 914 mm (36 in) across opposite flats and stands 1143 mm (45 in) tall, with 838 mm (33 in) headroom. You would be surprised at the size a child can fit into, so this play-house is not restricted to very young astronauts. Besides, squeezing into small spaces is part of the fun.

The capsule is an interesting shape to make, economical in its material requirements, and comprises two plug-together units, each hinged to fold in half, plus a nose cone and floor. They stand side by side and occupy very little storage space.

STAR RATING
Skill level **
Cost *
Child size **

MATERIALS

4 mm (³/₁₆ in) plywood:
1 sheet 2438 ×
1219 mm (8 × 4 ft)
1 half sheet 1219 ×
1219 mm (4 × 4 ft)
12 × 32 mm (½ × 1¼ in)
pine: 152 mm (6 in)
12 × 18 mm (½ × ¾ in)
pine: 8 at 863 mm
(34 in)
12 × 12 mm (½ in) pine:
2 at 813 mm (32 in)
18 mm (¾ in) ½ round
strip wood: 1143 mm
(45 in)
9 mm (³/₈ in) dowel:

914 mm (36 in)
6 mm (¼ in) dowel:
101 mm (4 in)
25 mm (1 in) strong
upholstery webbing:
762 mm (30 in)
2 spring-type wooden
clothes pegs
Panel pins
PVA glue
Glue sticks
Coat-hanger wire
Velcro pads
Abrasive paper
Filler
Non-toxic paint

TOOLS

- Hand saw or hand-held circular saw
- Hand-held jigsaw
- Tenon saw
- Plane
- Hammer
- Drill
- Scissors
- Glue gun
- Domestic iron
- Sanding block
- Pencil
- Rule
- Compass
- Try square
- Protractor
- Paint brushes

1 The main components fit tightly onto the plywood (Fig. 10.1). Mark them out carefully to avoid mistakes when cutting the many lines which are shared by pairs of components. First saw the sheet transversely into three sections, for ease of

Fig. 10.1

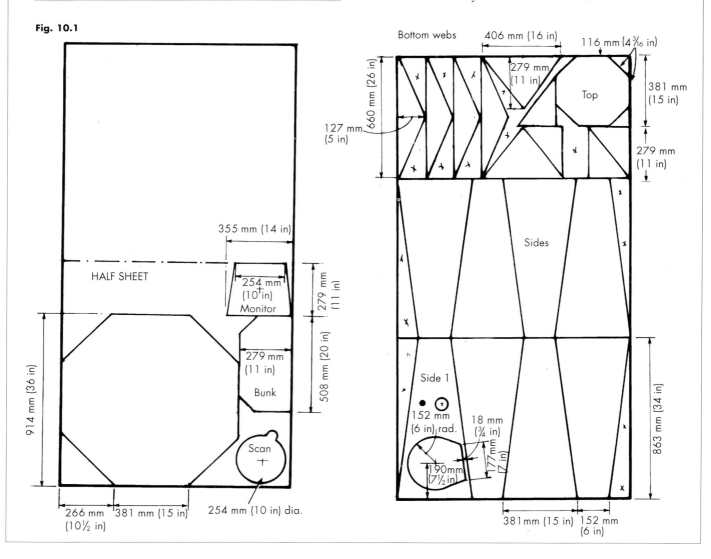

handling. Provided you follow the dimensions given, you should finish up with each of the two octagons being equal-sided. You can check this by drawing lines from corner to corner across a centre mark. This will show if one of the sides is incorrectly measured before you do the cutting. Note that only one side panel has the hatch and cherry-picker port. Save the waste areas for making packing pieces and small details.

Fig. 10.2

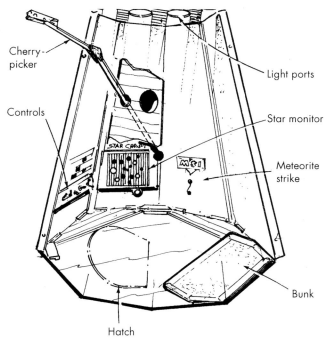

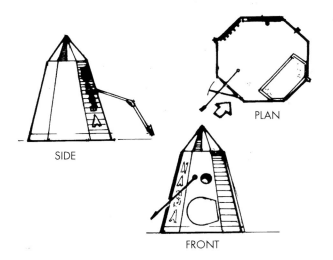

2 Number the side panels 1 to 8 starting with the one that has the hatch. Go counter-clockwise. Join them in pairs as seen in Fig. 10.3. Hinge the hatch cover, which is the waste piece from the hole. Use the webbing hinge method described in earlier projects and in Chapter 1.

Fig. 10.3

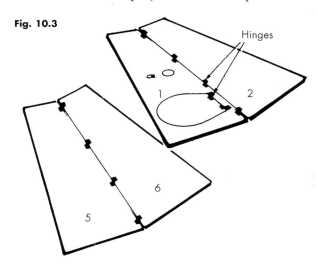

3 The pairs of hinged panels will be joined to form V-shaped sets. You join them on shaped strips, which you must plane to section. Fig. 10.4 shows how to mark out the chamfer lines before you plane to the sections shown. You will need four each of the double and single chamfered strips. The latter go outside and will be used to join the two assemblies with quick-detach dowels, as with the other projects. The panel numbering in Fig. 10.5 should make this clear.

Fig. 10.4

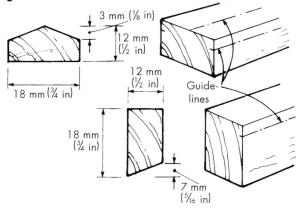

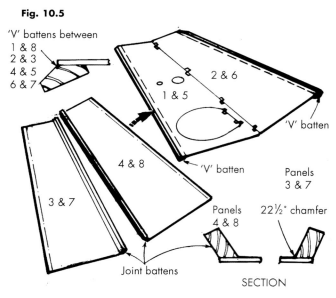

Fig. 10.5

'V' battens between
1 & 8
2 & 3
4 & 5
6 & 7

2 & 6

1 & 5

'V' batten

'V' batten

4 & 8

Panels
3 & 7

3 & 7

Panels
4 & 8

22½° chamfer

Joint battens

SECTION

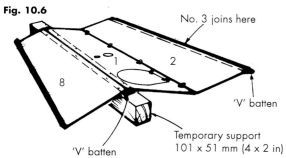

Fig. 10.6

No. 3 joins here

1

2

8

'V' batten

'V' batten

Temporary support
101 x 51 mm (4 x 2 in)

4 Lay the double-chamfered strips on a packing strip so that the side panels lie at a convenient angle for gluing and pinning (see Fig. 10.6). Turn the panels over carefully to avoid straining the joints while the glue is still wet, then clench the panel pin points over into the wood to avoid scratches and to prevent them loosening while the

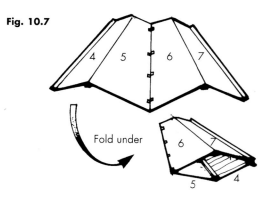

Fig. 10.7

4   5   6   7

Fold under

6   7

5   4

glue dries. It is best to do this on a hard flat surface or packing strip, with adjacent panels packed up, so as not to strain their joints too.

A finished set of four panels is shown in Fig. 10.7; note how it folds over to take up less space. Two such units make up the octagon.

5 Each V-shaped pair needs to be reinforced top and bottom. Each of the four bottom gussets which you cut from the plywood needs checking for angle and notching for the joining strip, as seen in Fig. 10.8.

Plane a chamfer, as shown in Fig. 10.9, on a strip of 12 × 12 mm (½ in) pine and cut it into sixteen pieces each 51 mm (2 in) long.

Fig. 10.8

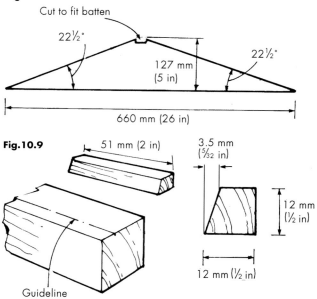

Cut to fit batten

22½°

127 mm
(5 in)

22½°

660 mm (26 in)

Fig.10.9

51 mm (2 in)

3.5 mm
(5/32 in)

12 mm
(½ in)

Guideline

12 mm (½ in)

Glue each gusset in the bottom edge of each pair of panels and glue the short reinforcing pieces in position along the junction of the gusset with the panels, as seen in Fig. 10.10. This will keep the bottom shape correct.

Fig.10.10

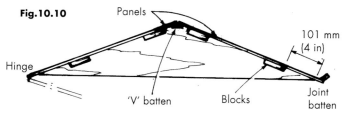

Panels

101 mm
(4 in)

Hinge

'V' batten

Blocks

Joint
batten

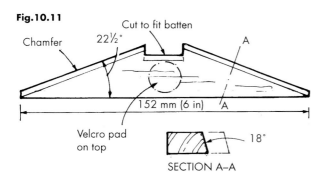

Fig.10.11

Chamfer

22½°

Cut to fit batten

A

152 mm (6 in)

A

Velcro pad on top

18°

SECTION A–A

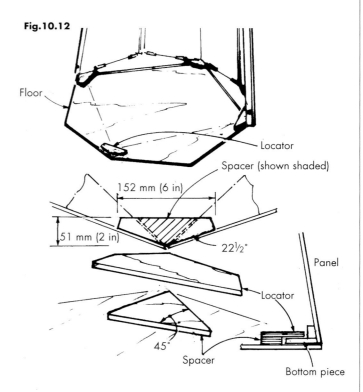

Fig.10.12

Floor

Locator

Spacer (shown shaded)

152 mm (6 in)

51 mm (2 in)

22½°

Panel

Locator

45°

Spacer

Bottom piece

6 Saw the top gussets from the small piece of 12 × 32 mm (½ × 1¼ in) pine, as in Fig. 10.11. Mark a line 3.5 mm (⁵⁄₃₂ in) back from the shaped edge and plane to a chamfer up to this line. Saw the notch back at the same angle to take the joiner strip. Make four of these and glue them in the top of the panels. They should lie horizontal when the two sets of panels are set up to form the octagon. Hold each piece in place with two G-cramps while the glue sets. (Do this singly if you have only two cramps.) Sand the tops level, and put a small pad of Velcro centrally to hold the nose cone in place.

7 Cut out the floor panel and rest one set of sides (half the enclosure) on it. The inside edges of the bottom gussets should be at right angles. Mark their positions on the floor, then remove the panels. Do the same with the opposite set of panels. You now have a guide line to show where to fix locating pieces which will retain the floor.

Fig. 10.12 shows the assembly of the locators and their position on the floor. The spacer pieces should be thicker than the gussets, so choose plywood that is the next grade up, or interpose a thinner piece or a strip of Formica or similar laminate to make up the thickness. Do not use cardboard – it will split.

When all four locators are in place, slide the panel units together so that the gussets slip under the locating plates. This will keep the shape symmetrical and the floor will not drop out if the capsule is lifted.

8 Make the nose cone as shown in Fig. 10.13. Cut eight 76 mm (3 in) holes opposite each flat on the small octagonal top panel. A hole saw will make short work of this, otherwise draw them with a compass and cut with the jigsaw. Draw a line from point to point across the centre, to use as a guide when positioning the triangular webs. Cut a slot in the bottom of one large triangle and one

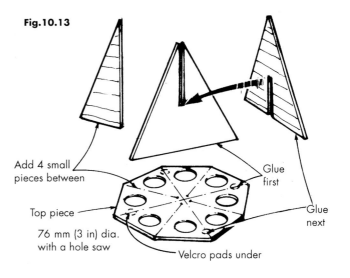

Fig.10.13

Add 4 small pieces between

Glue first

Top piece

Glue next

76 mm (3 in) dia. with a hole saw

Velcro pads under

in the top of the other. Each should go half way, as shown, to interlock.

Glue these together and to the top panel. There will be four right-angled triangles left. Glue these between the others to make eight webs. Put Velcro pads under the top panel to match their other halves on the top gussets of the main units. These will retain the nose cone, which you can remove by inserting a screwdriver in the joint and easing them apart.

9 Make the star monitor from two pieces of plywood or hardboard, to fit inside panel 6. Fig. 10.14 shows the construction. Use your own pattern for drilling the holes, but follow the method shown. The important part is to mark the position it will take on the panel and to match the taper on the sides to suit.

Fig. 10.14

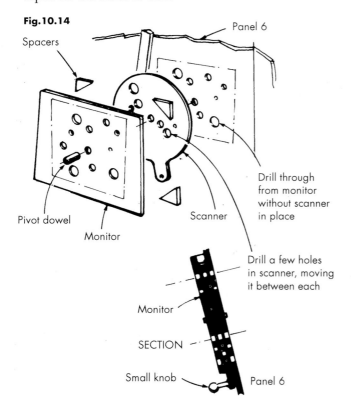

Spacers

Panel 6

Pivot dowel

Monitor

Scanner

Drill through from monitor without scanner in place

Monitor

SECTION

Small knob

Panel 6

Drill a few holes in scanner, moving it between each

Drill a centre hole 6 mm (¼ in) in diameter to take a pivot dowel of the same size. Use this to locate the components when you drill and reassemble after. Make only a few holes in the disk, as shown in the illustration. Paint all the parts matt black after drilling and sanding smooth, before gluing the pivot dowel to the screen and panel. As the disk is turned, different spots of light show, giving the effect of a scan.

10 The cherry-picker passes through a hole in panel 1. There is a small porthole near this point so that the operator can see where it is directed. Make this accessory as shown in Fig. 10.15. Use a G-cramp to hold the two plywood joiners to the dowels while the glue sets, then put in the staples. The hole in the panel should be large enough to allow the gripping end of the picker to get close to the entrance hatch, for collecting small items that have been retrieved.

Fig. 10.15

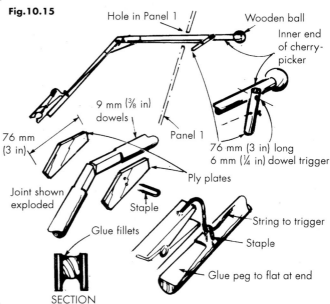

Hole in Panel 1

Wooden ball

Inner end of cherry-picker

9 mm (⅜ in) dowels

Panel 1

76 mm (3 in)

76 mm (3 in) long 6 mm (¼ in) dowel trigger

Ply plates

Joint shown exploded

Staple

String to trigger

Glue fillets

Staple

SECTION

Glue peg to flat at end

11 The sound effect of meteorites hitting the capsule is made by a piece of wood hitting the outside of panel 5. A spring clothes peg provides the action, opened by a string and allowed to snap shut. Fig. 10.16 shows the important gap in the peg jaws when at rest. This ensures that the piece of wood glued to the peg hits the panel before the peg has quite closed.

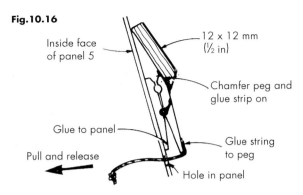

Fig. 10.16

Inside face of panel 5

12 x 12 mm (½ in)

Chamfer peg and glue strip on

Glue to panel

Glue string to peg

Pull and release

Hole in panel

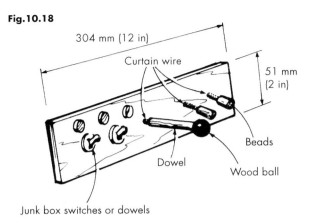

Fig. 10.18

304 mm (12 in)

Curtain wire

51 mm (2 in)

Beads

Dowel

Wood ball

Junk box switches or dowels

12 Make the bunk from the ply panel shown in Fig. 10.2. Glue on rounded strip to form an edge, as in Fig. 10.17. The bunk may be placed on the floor to suit the play theme. You can fix on thin foam of the type sold for putting under sleeping bags, or paint the bunk a contrasting colour.

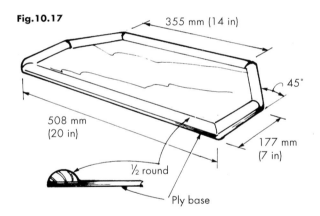

Fig. 10.17

355 mm (14 in)

45°

508 mm (20 in)

177 mm (7 in)

½ round

Ply base

13 Make the control panel from a plywood offcut and fix a collection of old switches, push buttons, slices of dowel, and short pieces of curtain wire with beads on the end, to represent

joysticks. Fig. 10.18 suggests the type of layout, but your intended astronauts may have a personal preference and can help with the customizing. Fix it on spacing blocks to panel 7.

14 Assemble the main panels together, put G-cramps on the edge strips and drill for the joiner dowels, as described in Chapter 1. You can glue triangular offcuts of plywood to these strips to represent fins.

15 Sand the capsule to round off sharp corners and edges. Put weatherproof tape over the two hinged joints to keep out unwanted light. Do this when the panels are folded, otherwise they will not fold fully.

Paint the inside a light grey, and the outside a darker metallic grey with alternate panels lighter. Add a serial number and other details in black.

If the capsule is to be taken into the garden, have a large plastic bucket handy to put over the nose cone if it rains, but see that it will be loose enough to allow plenty of air to reach the lighting holes.

Café

Eating out and tea parties are firm favourites in the list of children's play themes. Add a spot of cooking and a shop, and you have a café play-house. This project is a little larger than the others, so that benches and tables can be included. A service counter has a hob and microwave at the end. As you can see from Fig. 11.1, the large arched windows and vaulted roof give it a different appearance, for it might be a small 'under the railway arches' café in an industrial area, making an attempt to improve the scene with a window box and menu board.

The construction is similar to many of the other play-house projects and there is a full 1219 mm (48 in) headroom at the centre. It is 1219 × 1016 mm (48 × 40 in) and folds to only 254 mm (10 in) thick. The benches and tables can be taken outside where space permits, for a continental flavour, or used by themselves for other play themes.

STAR RATING
Skill level **
Cost ****
Child height *****

Fig. 11.1

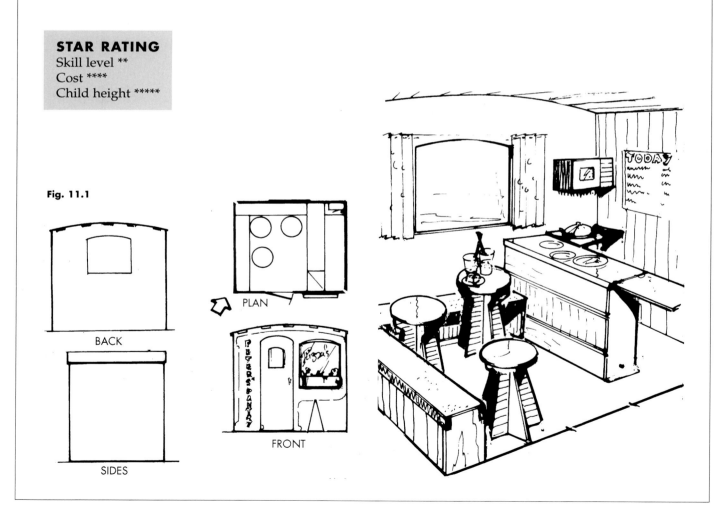

BACK

SIDES

PLAN

FRONT

MATERIALS

6 mm (¼ in) plywood: half
sheet – 1219 ×
1219 mm (48 in) –
or door size
4 mm (³/₁₆ in) plywood:
3 sheets 2438 ×
1219 mm (8 × 4 ft)
9 × 95 mm (³/₈ × 3¾ in)
pine: 2 at 152 mm (6 in)
9 × 63 mm (³/₈ × 2½ in)
pine: 4 at 762 mm
(30 in)
18 × 44 mm (¾ × 1¾ in)
pine: 1 at 686 mm
(27 in)
2 at 101 mm (4 in)
12 × 18 mm (½ × ¾ in)
pine: 5 at 1219 mm
(48 in)
4 at 1016 mm (40 in)
3 at 762 mm (30 in)
2 at 177 mm (7 in)
12 × 12 mm (½ in) pine:

1 at 762 mm (30 in)
2 at 609 mm (24 in)
4 at 177 mm (7 in)
9 mm (³/₈ in) dowel:
279 mm (11 in)
25 mm (1 in) strong
upholstery webbing:
1219 mm (48 in)
2 mm (³/₃₂ in) clear styrene
glazing: 1 at 406 ×
457 mm (16 × 18 in)
1 at 127 × 127 mm
(5 in)
4 at 25 mm (1 in) no. 10
roundhead woodscrews
PVA glue
Glue sticks
Panel pins
Abrasive paper
Coat-hanger wire
Cord
Filler
Non-toxic paint

TOOLS

- Hand saw or hand-held circular saw
- Hand-held jigsaw
- Tenon saw
- Drill
- Hammer
- Nail punch
- Pliers
- Glue gun
- Domestic iron
- Scissors
- Sanding block or sander
- Clothes pegs (for clamping)
- Rule
- Pencil
- Compass
- Try square

1 Mark out the three sheets of 4 mm (³/₁₆ in) plywood (see Fig. 11.3). To make the roof radius line, use a piece of batten with a nail in one end and the pencil in a hole or taped firmly to it near the other end, 1448 mm (57 in) from the nail. Extend a centre line past the end of the sheet onto a scrap piece of wood. Secure this and sweep the radius across. Check that the side dimension where it leaves the plywood is 1079 mm (42½ in) each side. If it is not, then the centre line is bent! Use a similar but smaller piece of wood and pencil to mark the window tops. Cut out all the panels with the hand saw or circular saw (for preference) and use the jigsaw on the curves and window cut-outs. Do not cut right across 'waste' areas, but preserve these long offcuts for division as indicated in Fig. 11.3.

2 Hinge each side to front and back panels as shown below. Do the door at the same time. Use webbing applied with the glue gun and iron it down for a good bond. The hinging technique is also shown in Chapter 1.

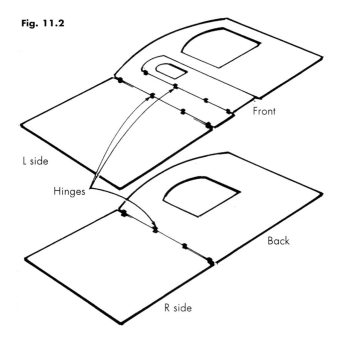

Fig. 11.2

Front

L side

Hinges

Back

R side

CAFÉ

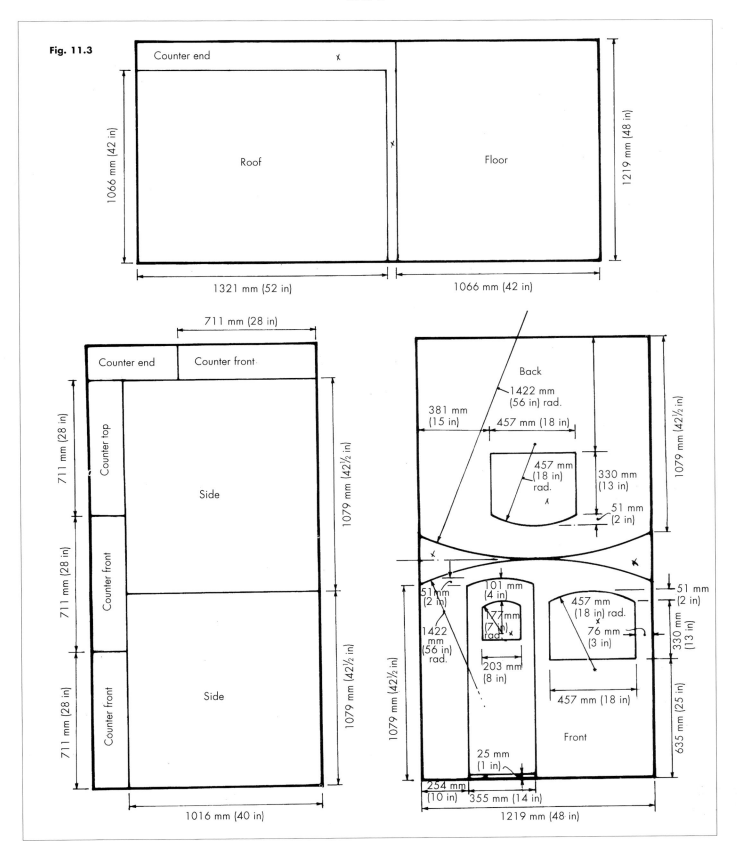

Fig. 11.3

Counter end

Roof

Floor

1066 mm (42 in)

1219 mm (48 in)

1321 mm (52 in)

1066 mm (42 in)

711 mm (28 in)

Counter end | Counter front

Counter top

711 mm (28 in)

Side

Counter front

711 mm (28 in)

1079 mm (42½ in)

Counter front

711 mm (28 in)

Side

1079 mm (42½ in)

1016 mm (40 in)

Back

1422 mm (56 in) rad.

381 mm (15 in)

457 mm (18 in)

457 mm (18 in) rad.

330 mm (13 in)

51 mm (2 in)

1079 mm (42½ in)

51 mm (2 in)

101 mm (4 in)

457 mm (18 in) rad.

1422 mm (56 in) rad.

177 mm (7 in) rad.

76 mm (3 in)

330 mm (13 in)

1079 mm (42½ in)

203 mm (8 in)

457 mm (18 in)

Front

635 mm (25 in)

25 mm (1 in)

254 mm (10 in)

355 mm (14 in)

1219 mm (48 in)

3 Glue and pin the edge strips to front and back of all four panels, as shown in Fig. 11.4. Note which strips are on edge and which are laid flat. Follow the key sketches and identity letters. Make up the jointed front strip as shown in Fig. 11.5, before fixing it to the panel. Clench any panel pin points before going further.

Fig. 11.4

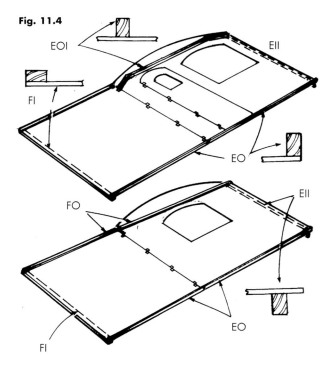

Fig. 11.5

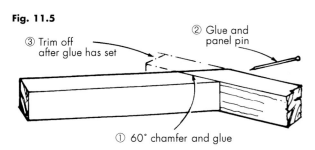

③ Trim off after glue has set

② Glue and panel pin

① 60° chamfer and glue

4 Using the window openings as a guide, mark out and cut narrow frame strips for the two large windows – see Fig. 11.6. They go on the outside and form a rebate. Glue them in place (no pins) and hold them with spring clothes pegs while the glue sets. Only the front window will be glazed with styrene, but save this until after painting, otherwise it will need masking.

Fig. 11.6

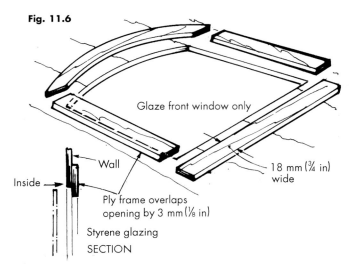

Glaze front window only

Wall

Inside

Ply frame overlaps opening by 3 mm (⅛ in)

Styrene glazing

SECTION

18 mm (¾ in) wide

5 Cut out the floor panel and arrange the two pairs of hinged walls on its edges. Bring the edge strips together and drill through both using a 9 mm (⅜ in) bit to take joining dowels, 76 mm (3 in) from top and bottom. Open out the holes in the outer strips and panels to clear, then glue the dowels onto the inner (recessed) strips. When set, reassemble and cross-drill the protruding dowels for wire locking pins. This technique also is illustrated in Chapter 1.

6 The roof panel is one rather flexible piece. It gains rigidity when you allow it to bend over the curved tops of the walls. To locate it there, glue 51 mm (2 in)-long strips of 12 × 12 mm (½ in) pine along each edge, as shown in Fig. 11.7. Drill two holes each end to fit over the heads of 25 mm (1 in) roundhead screws which you put into the top strips on each end wall while the roof is in position. You can then lift it off by easing it past the screwheads.

Fig. 11.7

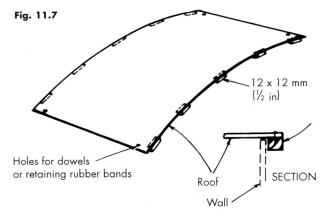

7 The service counter uses up the offcuts from some of the plywood, The outer grain goes in a different direction on one piece. Use this to advantage as shown in Fig. 11.8, when you assemble it with edge strips and a cover strip. One cross strip will support a shelf and joins two offcuts.

Make the counter ends as shown in Fig. 11.9. Note that one end plugs into holes in the back wall and the other is shorter, to sit on a locating piece which you glue to the floor panel. Position the end panel against the back wall, 228 mm (9 in) from the side and drill through for the dowels, before

Fig. 11.8

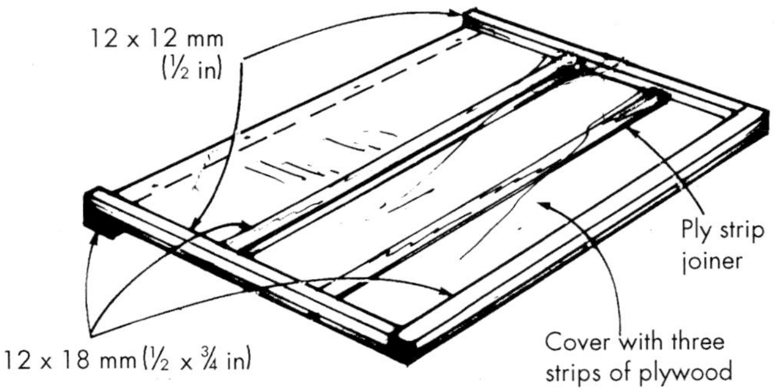

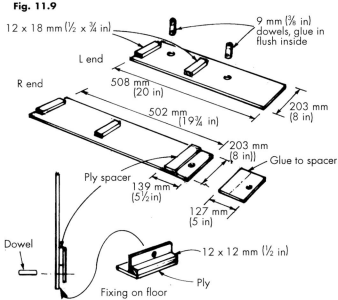

Fig. 11.9

you glue the dowels into the end panel, or fit the latter to the counter.

Cut the counter top and flap and hinge them together with webbing as in Fig. 11.10. Make a shelf from other plywood offcuts and glue it onto the supports underneath the counter top, also glue a strip of wood to the front wall where the flap can rest.

Fig. 11.10

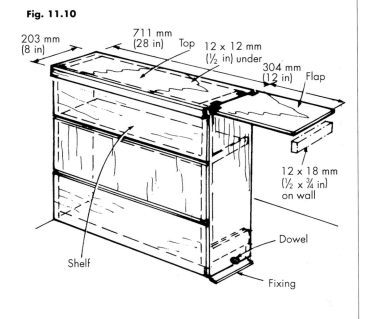

8 Glue another strip to the end wall behind the counter to support a hob panel. Cut the latter from a ply offcut and glue a strip of 12 × 18 mm (½ × ¾ in) pine on edge underneath, but inset from the end. Check that the hob end rests on the counter top, as in Fig. 11.11. If you have positioned the counter further than 228 mm (9 in) from the wall (Fig. 11.10) it has to be larger. Glue on some slices of dowel to represent controls.

Fig. 11.11

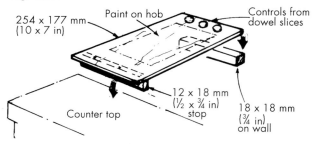

254 × 177 mm (10 × 7 in)
Paint on hob
Controls from dowel slices
12 × 18 mm (½ × ¾ in) stop
18 × 18 mm (¾ in) on wall
Counter top

9 Make the microwave from 4 mm (³⁄₁₆ in) plywood or hardboard glued onto end pieces of 9 × 95 mm (⅜ × 3¾ in) pine. The dimensions are shown in Fig. 11.12. Hinge the door to the narrow flap before you assemble the latter to the end. Cut

Fig. 11.12

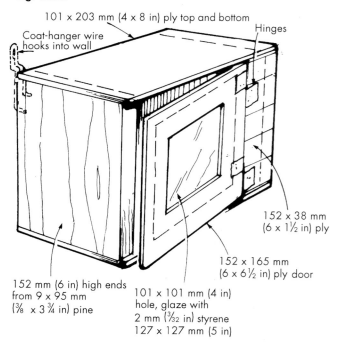

101 × 203 mm (4 × 8 in) ply top and bottom
Coat-hanger wire hooks into wall
Hinges
152 × 38 mm (6 × 1½ in) ply
152 × 165 mm (6 × 6½ in) ply door
152 mm (6 in) high ends from 9 × 95 mm (⅜ × 3¾ in) pine
101 × 101 mm (4 in) hole, glaze with 2 mm (³⁄₃₂ in) styrene 127 × 127 mm (5 in)

a piece of styrene glazing for the door, but do not fix (with the glue gun) until after painting. Make a pair of hooks from coat-hanger wire and glue and tape them (with webbing) to the top back corners. Drill matching holes in the back wall. The microwave has to be unhooked before folding the walls up for storage.

10 You will need two bench seats and three tables. Make these from the 6 mm (¼ in) plywood; Fig. 11.13 gives the dimensions and details. You can glue and pin into the edges of this thicker plywood, but additional strength is provided by 12 × 12 mm (½ in) strips glued in the angle between end and top. Two 9 × 63 mm (⅜ × 2½ in) rails take the weight and steady the ends.

Fig. 11.13

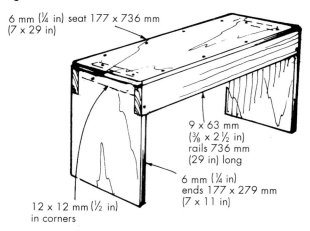

6 mm (¼ in) seat 177 × 736 mm (7 × 29 in)
9 × 63 mm (⅜ × 2½ in) rails 736 mm (29 in) long
6 mm (¼ in) ends 177 × 279 mm (7 × 11 in)
12 × 12 mm (½ in) in corners

11 The table tops are hinged to one leg panel, and the other leg panel slots dry, into the first, to keep the top level. They can thus be folded up for storage. All the dimensions are given in Fig. 11.14, which also shows the method of assembly from flat. Make a firm job of the hinging to avoid wobble on the top.

Fig. 11.14

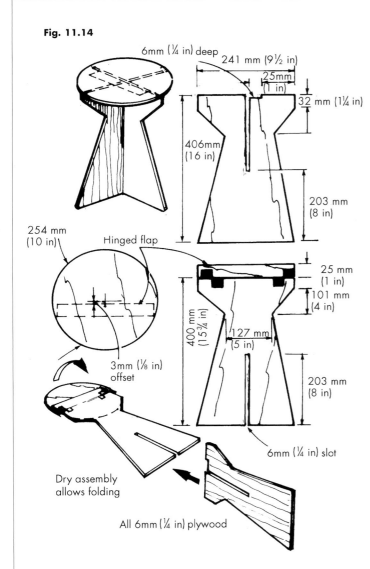

6mm (¼ in) deep

241 mm (9½ in)

25mm (1 in)

32 mm (1¼ in)

406mm (16 in)

203 mm (8 in)

254 mm (10 in)

Hinged flap

3mm (⅛ in) offset

400 mm (15¾ in)

127 mm (5 in)

25 mm (1 in)

101 mm (4 in)

203 mm (8 in)

6mm (¼ in) slot

Dry assembly allows folding

All 6mm (¼ in) plywood

Fig. 11.15

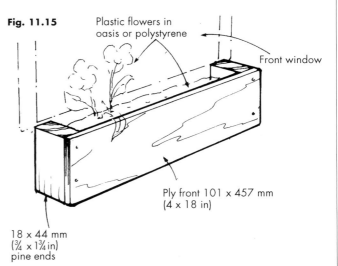

Plastic flowers in oasis or polystyrene

Front window

Ply front 101 x 457 mm (4 x 18 in)

18 x 44 mm (¾ x 1¾ in) pine ends

12 Dress up the front window with a simple flower box, as shown in Fig. 11.15. It needs no bottom or back – just glue and pin the strip of plywood offcut to two 101 mm (4 in) pieces of 18 × 44 mm (¾ × 1¾ in) pine and glue these to the wall under the window frame. Wedge in a piece of expanded polystyrene and 'plant' it with artificial flowers.

13 An outdoor menu board can add atmosphere. Two hinged hardboard panels suitably painted, will not take you long to make (see Fig. 11.16). Join them with a cord. The children will enjoy chalking up the fayre of the day.

Fig. 11.16

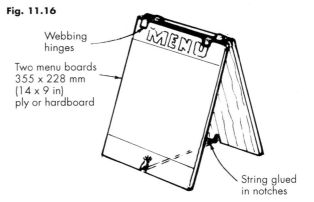

Webbing hinges

MENU

Two menu boards 355 x 228 mm (14 x 9 in) ply or hardboard

String glued in notches

14 Finish off by sanding all corners and edges smooth and filling small hollows and areas of open grain. Paint light bright colours inside and out, although you can make a feature of the contrasting wood grain on the counter front by varnishing it clear. Give the hob fluorescent orange paper stripes on black. Have the roof dark grey outside so as to look like asphalt, but keep lettering bold on the front. You can also paint some lettering or a logo on the glazing before you fix it into the front window frame, as the last job.

Saloon

Spooky Creek Saloon is a play-house for the young cowboys in the family. There is a hitching rail for bikes, an open doorway with short Mexican-style swing doors, and an angled front to give more room there. As you can see from Fig. 12.1, the saloon tapers to a crowded area around the old piano, and there is an escape door behind the bar for hasty exits. The mirror behind the bar is unbreakable and shows who is hiding in the corner before you 'go bustin' in'. Two stools and a table complete the scene; unlike those in westerns, these are not intended to be breakable!

   The angled wall presents no constructional problems, because it is hinged to the side wall, and can take up the slight difference in the other joint. The play-house folds from a maximum of 1016 mm (40 in) deep and wide to 355 mm (14 in) deep, or 254 mm (10 in) less if the furniture is stacked elsewhere, or used as separate playthings. The headroom is a full 1219 mm (48 in) at the ridge.

STAR RATING
Skill level **
Cost ****
Child height *****

MATERIALS

6 mm (¼ in) plywood: half
sheet – 1219 × 1219 mm
(48 in)

4 mm (³⁄₁₆ in) plywood:
3 sheets 2438 ×
1219 mm (8 × 4 ft)

18 × 44 mm (¾ × 1¾ in)
pine: 762 mm (30 in)

12 × 76 mm (½ × 3 in)
pine: 1 at 431 mm (17 in)

12 × 51 mm (½ × 2 in)
pine: 1 at 431 mm (17 in)
2 at 711 mm (28 in)

12 × 18 mm (½ × ¾ in)
pine: 4 at 1219 mm
(48 in)
2 at 1041 mm (41 in)
4 at 1016 mm (40 in)
2 at 787 mm (31 in)
2 at 686 mm (27 in)
2 at 203 mm (8 in)

12 × 12 mm (½ in) pine:
1 at 1041 mm (41 in)

1 at 813 mm (32 in)
2 at 635 mm (25 in)
2 at 559 mm (22 in)
2 at 381 mm (15 in)
3 at 241 mm (9½ in)
8 at 76 mm (3 in)

18 mm (¾ in) dowel:
584 mm (23 in)

9 mm (³⁄₈ in) dowel:
406 mm (16 in)

25 mm (1 in) strong
upholstery webbing:
1295 mm (51 in)

Spring curtain wire:
152 mm (6 in)

4 small staples
Chrome heat-shrink film
Panel pins
PVA glue
Glue sticks
Abrasive paper
Non-toxic paint

TOOLS

- Hand saw or hand-held circular saw
- Tenon saw
- Hand-held jigsaw
- Chisel
- Drill
- Pliers
- Hammer
- Nail punch
- Glue gun
- Domestic iron
- Hair drier
- Scissors
- Paint brushes
- Pencil
- Rule
- Try square

Fig. 12.1

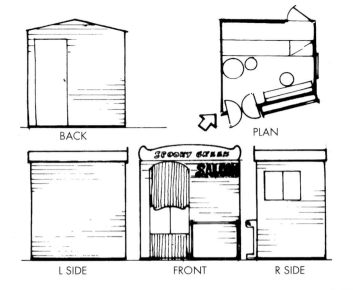

BACK   PLAN

L SIDE   FRONT   R SIDE

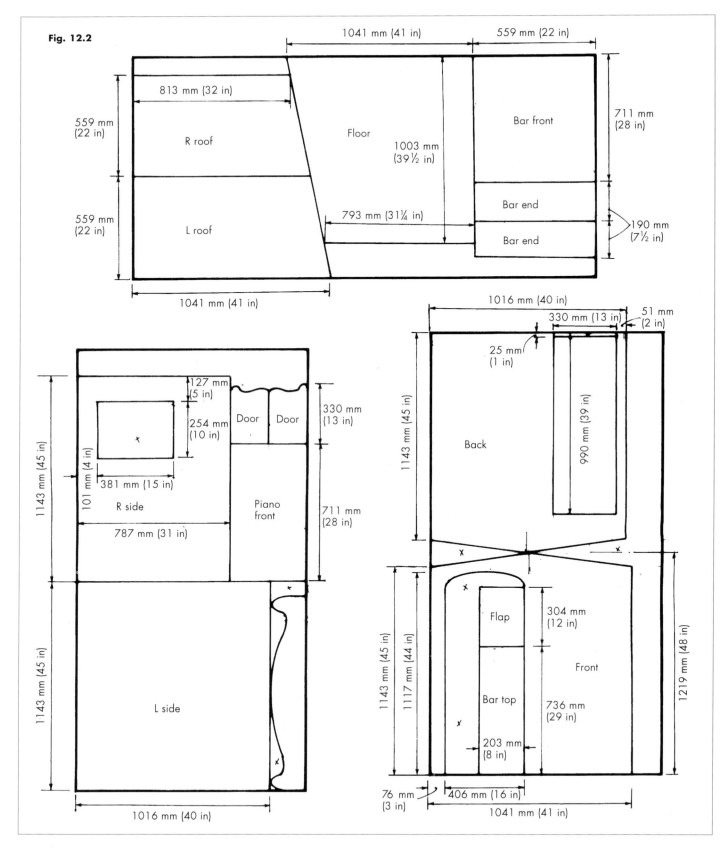

Fig. 12.2

1 Fig. 12.2 shows the main components on the three large sheets of plywood. Follow this pattern when you mark them out. The dimensions allow for saw cuts, so make the line central on each dimension. Several panels share the same cutting line, which saves time. Small parts like the doors and nameplate are detailed separately. The remaining areas are not all waste – in fact you should save these as they are drawn, for cutting small parts later. For this reason, do not saw through long areas, but keep them stored flat until needed.

2 Work on the floor with a thick batten under the plywood near the intended cutting line. This will space the circular saw blade and guard clear of the floor. Move along the sheet and join up straight cuts for the doorways with the jigsaw, always keeping the packing strip near the line but not in the way of the blade. Drill two holes diagonally in the window opening and use the jigsaw to cut towards the remaining corners. Fig. 12.3 shows the shape of the tops of the swing doors. Draw grid lines to help you to mark it out for this more detailed cutting. Leave the precise marking and cutting of the nameplate for the moment. Fig. 12.2 shows the position rather than the exact shape.

Fig. 12.3

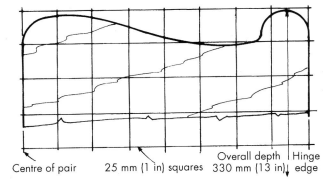

Centre of pair   25 mm (1 in) squares   Overall depth 330 mm (13 in) | Hinge edge

3 Lay out the front and right wall panels and the swing doors and join them with webbing hinges (clothes horse fashion), as described in other projects and in Chapter 1. Note the distance of the doors from the bottom edge, shown in Fig. 12.4. Continue with the other two wall panels and back door, shown in the same diagram. It is important to work on a flat surface while fixing the hinges.

Fig. 12.4

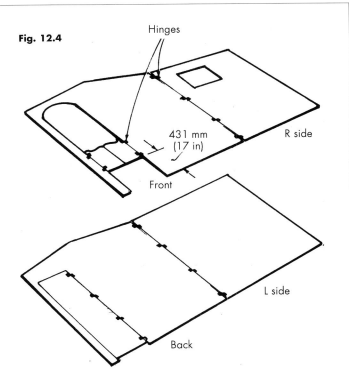

Hinges

431 mm (17 in)

Front

R side

L side

Back

4 Now select strips of 12 × 18 mm (½ × ¾ in) pine of the correct lengths, and glue and pin them to the inner and outer faces where shown in Fig. 12.5. Note which are flat, and which are on edge; the key sections will help you here. Clench

Fig. 12.5

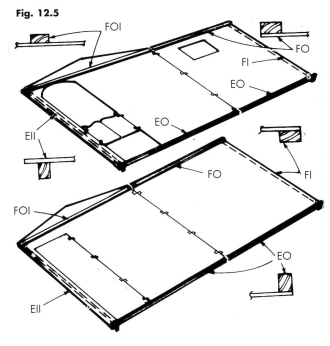

FOI

FO

FI

EO

EO

EII

FO

FI

FOI

EO

EII

Fig. 12.6

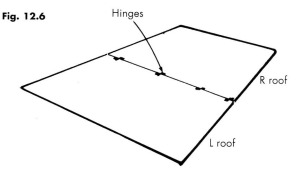

Hinges

R roof

L roof

the points of any panel pins that protrude through the flat strips. Make sure that the points go below the surface after the pins have been beaten over. Use the nail punch here. With chisel and glass-paper, round off the top edges of the bottom strip where it crosses the openings of front and back doors. Do NOT cut it away completely; it is needed to prevent the panels warping.

Put the two pairs of panels aside so that they are not twisted, then hinge the roof panels as in Fig. 12.6, using the same technique. Continue as in Fig. 12.7, by gluing and pinning strips of 12 x 12 mm (½ in) pine under the outer edges. Chamfer the centre ends of front and back strips to allow the roof to adopt the correct slope (pitch). It will fold right over the opposite way for convenient storage.

Fig. 12.7

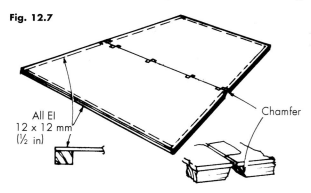

All El
12 × 12 mm
(½ in)

Chamfer

5 Using the shorter strips of 12 × 12 mm (½ in) pine, form the window frame for the right-hand panel. Lightly groove the outer edges of four strips to fit over the edge of the plywood; 1.5 mm (¹⁄₁₆ in) is adequate. You can use the tenon saw and chisel for this, or a plough plane if you have one. The groove helps to hold the frame central in the opening. Fit the top and bottom strips first – they need end grooves too. Now trim to length and glue in the sides and an ungrooved centre strip (see Fig. 12.8).

Fig. 12.8

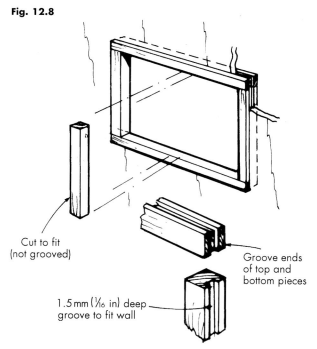

Cut to fit
(not grooved)

Groove ends
of top and
bottom pieces

1.5 mm (¹⁄₁₆ in) deep
groove to fit wall

6 The swing doors will be flopping about on their hinges. Bring some order in here; make small notches in the frame as shown in Fig. 12.9 and kink one end of a piece of curtain spring. Bend it over less sharply further up, so that it adopts a gentle right-angled bend, as shown. Secure it with a staple which goes over the door frame and another over the door. The staples should not be so tight that the spring cannot twist and slide a little. Secure the staples by first pinch-ing with the pliers, then fix them both, and the kinked end of the spring, with the glue gun. Do not put glue (or thick paint) on the other part of

Fig. 12.9

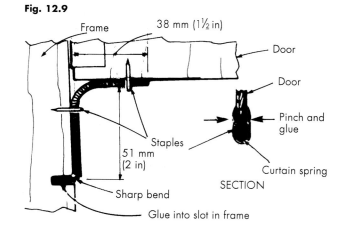

Frame

38 mm (1½ in)

Door

Door

Pinch and
glue

Staples

51 mm
(2 in)

Curtain spring

SECTION

Sharp bend

Glue into slot in frame

the spring. The door should now close centrally after opening either way. Repeat the exercise on the other door. The doors should not touch where they meet.

7 The nameplate is shown gridded in Fig. 12.10. This is a half-view; set it out on the plywood using 25 mm (1 in) squares, then draw it left- and right-handed on a straight bottom line, that is the edge of the sheet.

Smooth the edges and glue and pin it along its bottom edge to the top strip in the front panel. Also glue a small spacing strip of the same section 18 mm (¾ in) below the top of the gable.

Fig. 12.10

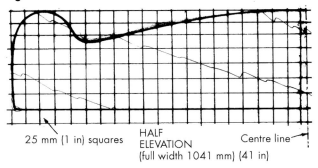

25 mm (1 in) squares   HALF ELEVATION (full width 1041 mm) (41 in)   Centre line

8 Cut out the counter front, and, following Fig. 12.11, glue and pin the edge strips in place. It is shown face-downwards here. Continue by making the two ends of the counter as shown in Fig. 12.12. Note that the right-hand end is shorter, to seat on a locating piece which you glue to the floor panel when you have positioned the finished counter.

Mark a vertical line 254 mm (10 in) from the back edge of the left side wall. Now lay the back

Fig. 12.12

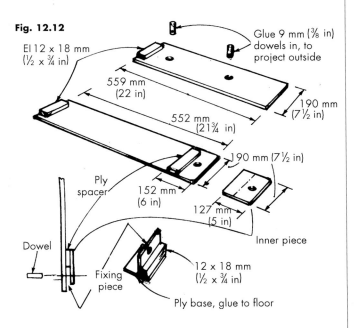

El 12 x 18 mm (½ x ¾ in)
Glue 9 mm (⅜ in) dowels in, to project outside
559 mm (22 in)
552 mm (21¾ in)
190 mm (7½ in)
190 mm (7½ in)
Ply spacer
152 mm (6 in)
127 mm (5 in)
Inner piece
Dowel
Fixing piece
12 x 18 mm (½ x ¾ in)
Ply base, glue to floor

edge of the left counter end against it. Drill through the holes and through the wall. Glue 9 mm (⅜ in) dowels into the counter end to locate in the wall.

Assemble the counter with glue and panel pins, adding the top with hinged flap and a foot rail, all as shown in Fig. 12.13.

Fig. 12.11

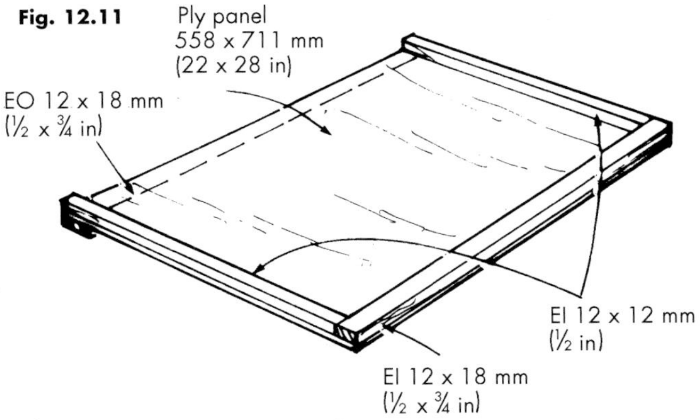

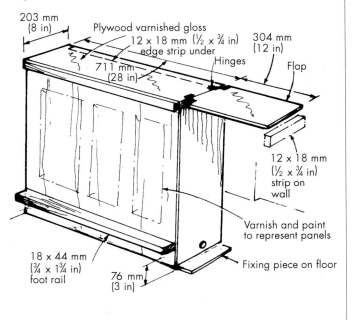

Ply panel 558 x 711 mm (22 x 28 in)
EO 12 x 18 mm (½ x ¾ in)
El 12 x 12 mm (½ in)
El 12 x 18 mm (½ x ¾ in)

Fig. 12.13

203 mm (8 in)
Plywood varnished gloss
12 x 18 mm (½ x ¾ in) edge strip under
304 mm (12 in)
711 mm (28 in)
Hinges
Flap
12 x 18 mm (½ x ¾ in) strip on wall
18 x 44 mm (¾ x 1¾ in) foot rail
76 mm (3 in)
Varnish and paint to represent panels
Fixing piece on floor

9 Place the hinged back and left side walls to the edge of the floor panel, plug the counter into the side wall and make it parallel to the back wall. Glue the locating piece to the floor while it is in the slot in the right-hand end of the counter.

10 Disconnect the counter, lay the back wall on the floor and measure the counter height from the bottom. Above this line form a narrow frame from four strips of plywood. Glue these to the back wall, as in Fig. 12.14. Smooth them carefully and apply chrome heat-shrink film, to the edges only, with the domestic iron. This material is sold in model shops for use on model aeroplanes. Fixing instructions come with it. Tighten the film with a hair drier after fixing it all round. Take care not to press it onto the wall near the centre. The result of a properly tightened area of film will be an unbreakable mirror. If it is accidentally pressed, the reflection will distort in an interesting way, only to recover again. Do not apply the film directly to a large flat surface; any slight texture will prevent it reflecting like a mirror.

11 Fig. 12.14 also shows a dummy shelf under the mirror. Make this from a strip of plywood with a spacing strip of plastic laminate off-cut along the bottom.

This forms a groove into which the bar tender can push cardboard cut-outs of bottles. The bottles reflect in the mirror and give the effect of depth.

12 No saloon is complete without the old piano that seems to keep on playing in spite of any shoot-outs that are going on. The one in Fig. 12.15 is a dummy, although a small tape recorder might be incorporated under the painted keyboard.

Make a frame from the three strips of 12 × 51 mm (½ × 2 in) pine and glue the front panel on to them. Glue and pin a pair of plywood side shapes in place, then fit and glue the 12 × 76 mm (½ × 3 in) pine 'keyboard' between. There is no back to the piano. Add two dowels to locate it in the front wall (mark and drill this to match). Position the front wall to the floor and put the piano in place. Glue two short pieces of strip as shown. These piano pedals serve to locate the bottom of the piano.

Fig. 12.14

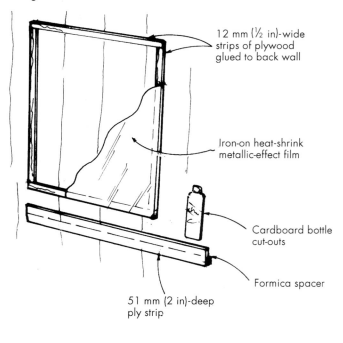

12 mm (½ in)-wide strips of plywood glued to back wall

Iron-on heat-shrink metallic-effect film

Cardboard bottle cut-outs

Formica spacer

51 mm (2 in)-deep ply strip

Fig. 12.15

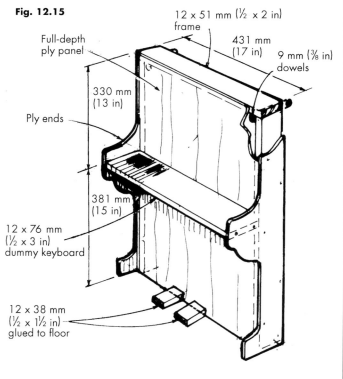

12 x 51 mm (½ × 2 in) frame

431 mm (17 in)

9 mm (⅜ in) dowels

Full-depth ply panel

330 mm (13 in)

Ply ends

381 mm (15 in)

12 x 76 mm (½ x 3 in) dummy keyboard

12 x 38 mm (½ x 1½ in) glued to floor

Fig. 12.16

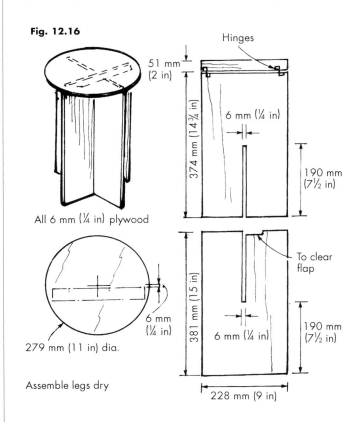

51 mm (2 in)

Hinges

374 mm (14¾ in)

6 mm (¼ in)

190 mm (7½ in)

All 6 mm (¼ in) plywood

279 mm (11 in) dia.

6 mm (¼ in)

Assemble legs dry

To clear flap

381 mm (15 in)

6 mm (¼ in)

190 mm (7½ in)

228 mm (9 in)

13 Make the table and two stools from the 6 mm (¼ in) plywood. Fig. 12.16 shows how you slot the two rectangular leg pieces together without any glue. One has a hinged flap which you glue under the table top. The table takes to pieces for storage, but may well appear to be broken in the excitement. The stools (Fig. 12.17)

Fig. 12.17

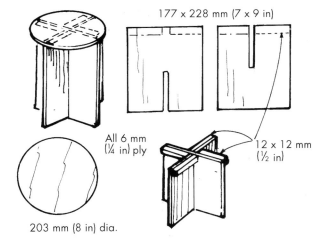

177 x 228 mm (7 x 9 in)

All 6 mm (¼ in) ply

12 x 12 mm (½ in)

203 mm (8 in) dia.

have to be more rigid and have glued joints throughout. Pieces of 12 × 12 mm (½ in) pine give extra gluing area for the seat disks.

14 The hitching rail outside the front wall folds flat for storage and is kept extended by inserting the dowel rail, as shown in Fig. 12.18. Hinge both the rail supports to narrow flaps which you then glue to the wall. The rail has plywood washers glued near each end. Cross-drill the ends for locking pins made from coat-hanger wire, just as detailed in the quick-detach joints used for the two corners of the play-house itself.

Fig. 12.18

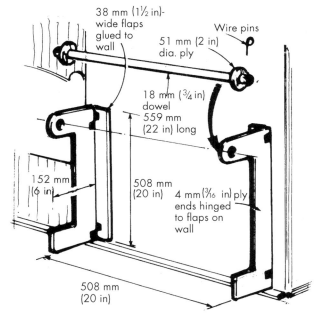

38 mm (1½ in)-wide flaps glued to wall

Wire pins

51 mm (2 in) dia. ply

18 mm (¾ in) dowel 559 mm (22 in) long

152 mm (6 in)

508 mm (20 in)

4 mm (³⁄₁₆ in) ply ends hinged to flaps on wall

508 mm (20 in)

15 Finish all by sanding corners and sharp edges, smoothing and filling open grain and other blemishes. Varnish the bar front and add paint lines to represent wood panelling. Varnish the counter until shiny, so that drinks can be slid along it in the approved manner. Varnish and dirty-up the piano, add posters and a stuffed moose head made from felt and cardboard. Use white or cream paint on the walls and ceiling, and white outside, with horizontal lines painted on to look like clapboard. Paint the roof a rusty shade, and decorate the front with black lettering on the nameplate and wall.

Station

Watch a youngster on a trundle engine or on a little tricycle, as he or she makes train noises. There is something missing, in the play room or on the patio. Yes, it is the railway station, where one can be station-master, ticket-collector, and work in the signal-box. This compact play-house has all these facilities, plus a platform and a waiting-room. There is a signal worked by one of the levers in the signal-box part of the ticket office, and a fancy valance sets off the platform canopy, in the style of an old country station – let us call it FROGLEY.

To complete the picture, there are details of a dummy railway coach compartment, which is like a piece of stage scenery. Passengers can push this alongside the platform and alight or board the 'train' via its door. There is scope for many role changes if one, two or more children are using the finished project, which is shown in Fig. 13.1.

The two 508 mm (20 in)-wide compartments are a full 1219 mm (48 in) high at the ridge and 1117 mm (44 in) at the eaves. Windows in the signal cabin part give views up and down the platform, there is a door with a ticket window in the partition and an entrance door to the station waiting-room. An archway leads to the platform; when the ticket door is open, it forms a barrier.

When the station is stored against a wall, it is about 250 mm (10 in) deep. Fully extended for play, the platform is 1422 mm (56 in) long, and the depth to the back wall is 1219 mm (48 in).

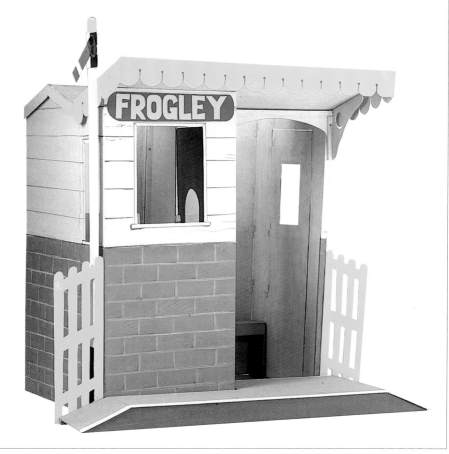

STAR RATING
Skill rating **
Cost ***
Child height ****

MATERIALS

4 mm (³/₁₆ in) plywood:
  3 sheets 2438 ×
  1219 mm (8 × 4 ft)
18 × 89 mm (¾ × 3½ in)
  pine: 2 at 1524 mm
  (60 in)
  1 at 381 mm (15 in)
32 × 32 mm (1¼ in)
  pine:1828 mm (72 in)
12 × 51 mm (½ × 2 in)
  pine: 4 at 381 mm
  (15 in)
  4 at 127 mm (5 in)
12 × 18 mm (½ × ¾ in)
  pine: 2 at 1219 mm
  (48 in)
  1 at 1117 mm (44 in)
  2 at 1016 mm (40 in)
  6 at 609 mm (24 in)
  2 at 457 mm (18 in)
12 × 12 mm (½ in) pine:
  2 at 1219 mm (48 in)
  2 at 1066 mm (42 in)
  6 at 330 mm (13 in)
9 mm (⅜ in) dowel:
  406 mm (16 in)
25 mm (1 in)-wide strong
  upholstery webbing:
  2590 mm (102 in)

String
Coat-hanger wire
4 at 51 mm (2 in) no. 8
  roundhead woodscrews
20 mm (¾ in) panel pins
PVA glue
Glue sticks
Abrasive paper
Paint
Large empty paint drum or
  beer can

For the carriage accessory
you will need the
following extras:
4 mm (³/₁₆ in) plywood:
  1117 × 1117 mm
  (44 in)
12 × 18 mm (½ × ¾ in)
  pine: 2 at 1117 mm
  (44 in)
  2 at 1371 mm (54 in)
4 small wheels and
  screws for axles
2 plastic drawer handles
Webbing: 304 mm
  (12 in)
2 weights (short pieces of
  garden stone coping)

TOOLS

- Hand saw or hand-held
  circular saw
- Hand-held jigsaw
- Tenon saw
- Chisel
- Plane
- Drill
- Screwdriver
- Hammer
- Nail punch
- Glue gun
- Domestic iron
- Try square
- Rule
- Pencil
- Compass
- Scissors
- Sanding block or
  sander
- Paint brushes

1 Mark out the parts on the sheets of plywood. Mark each for identification, following the layout in Fig. 13.2. Note that there are two sets of platform pieces. You will laminate these pairs to make a strong surface (this saves you buying a whole sheet of thicker plywood for these items alone).

Lay each of the whole panels on the floor with a strip of 76 × 51 mm (3 × 2 in) sawn timber

Fig. 13.1

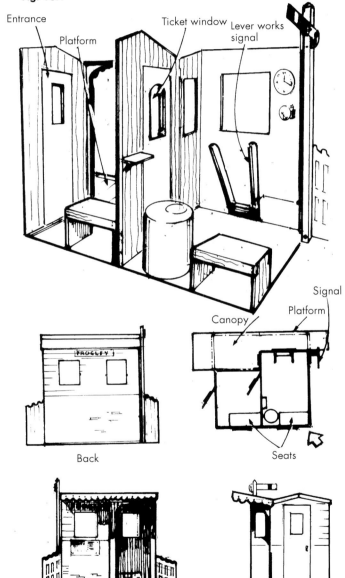

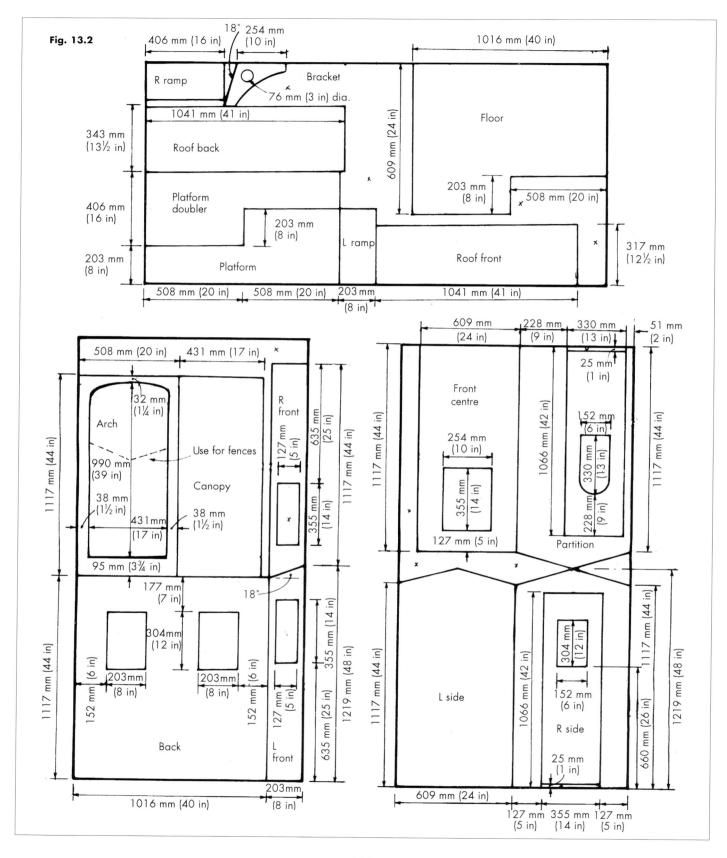

Fig. 13.2

underneath, near the cutting line. This will give clearance for the tip of the hand saw, or the guard and blade of the circular saw. Make the straight cuts and join them at the tops of doors, by drilling a hole and cutting across with the jigsaw. Drill in the corners of windows, and make two cuts from each with the jigsaw. Support the wood near the cut when doing this, otherwise there will be a lot of vibration and not much accuracy.

2 The small sloping fence pieces, which will go at each end of the building come next. Mark out these as shown in Fig. 13.3 and drill a hole in the diagonally opposite corners of each cut-out. Support the work on the edge of the bench or on the spacing strip, as you did with the main panels, then shape the top edge and form the nine slots with the jigsaw. Clean up the cut edges and repeat for the second fence.

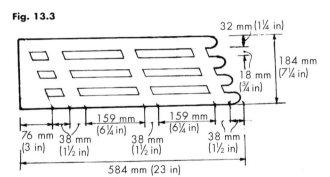

Fig. 13.3

3 Smooth the cut edges and lay out the sets of panels on the floor. Tackle each set in turn. The complete arrangement is shown in Fig. 13.4.

Cut 52 pieces of webbing, each 38 mm (1½ in) long. These will form the hinges which join the components. Fix them alternately to each side of the hinge line with the glue gun, and smooth with the iron set on full heat. Hinging is shown in Chapter 1. When you have hinged all five sets of pieces, they are ready for reinforcement.

4 Fig. 13.5 shows the positions of the fourteen pine strips of 12 × 18 mm (½ × ¾ in) and two of 12 × 12 mm (½ in), which you now glue and pin to the panels. Do all the strips that are on the inner faces first, as shown dotted, then after marking, turn each set over and fix the outside strip, which will now be underneath.

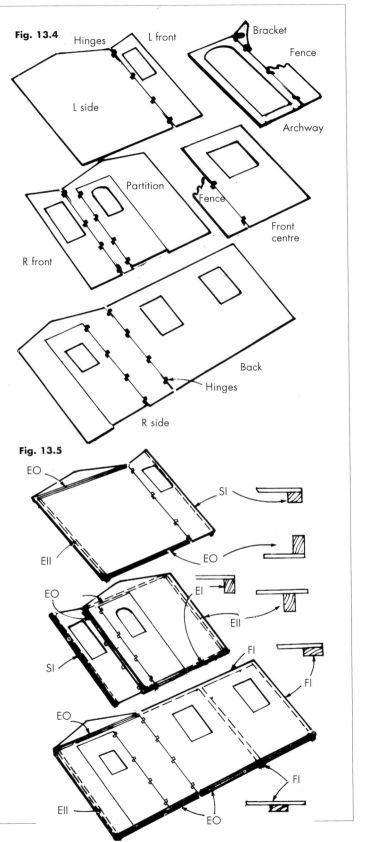

Fig. 13.4

Fig. 13.5

When you finally pick up the sets of panels, remember to fold them inner face to inner face, otherwise the outer strips will clash and strain the hinges. The play-houses are all designed to be folded in this way so that less space is taken up when opening them out for assembly.

5 Complete the reinforcement by adding strips to the archway panel as in Fig. 13.6. Note that they do not run right to the edges. This is to allow for adjacent strips already on the other pieces.

The projecting bay of the signal-box part has to be rigidly assembled, so following the main part of Fig. 13.6, fold the side panels out of the way and use a heavy strip of packing wood to support the 12×12 mm ($\frac{1}{2}$ in) strips already on the narrow

Fig. 13.7

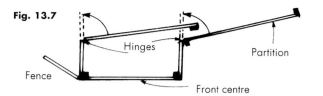

Fig. 13.8

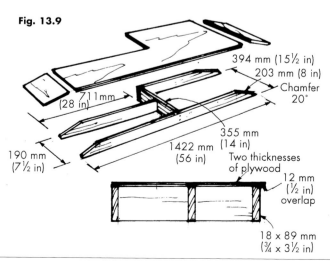

panels. Glue and pin the front panel in place. It has no strips at top or bottom because the canopy and platform will support it. Fig. 13.7 shows how the main side and partition hinge out to form the full assembly plan view in Fig. 13.8. The back and right side assembly will be secured with two quick-detach dowel fittings at the back corner and at the partition. The arch panel joins the front corner to the partition at the top with similar dowels.

6 Make the platform as shown in Fig. 13.9. Start by gluing the pairs of ply panels together to

Fig. 13.6

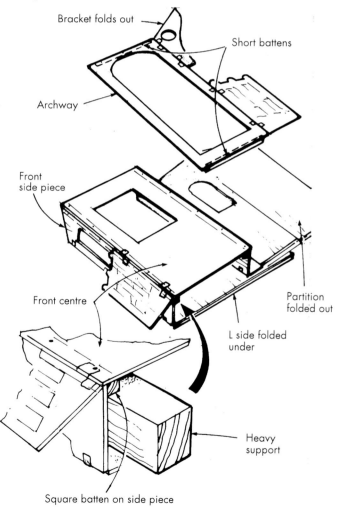

Fig. 13.9

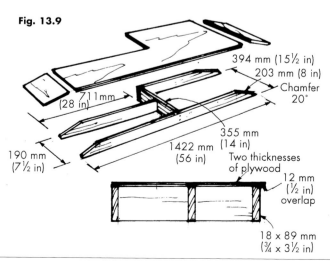

make double-thickness pieces. Place them on a flat surface and put weights on top while the glue sets. Meanwhile, saw the end shapes on the pieces of 18 × 89 mm (¾ × 3½ in) pine. All the dimensions are shown in the diagram. Glue and nail these pieces together, checking that they are square with the try square.

Now chamfer the meeting edges of the main and end platform panels so that they fit together evenly, then glue and pin them to the pine framework with an overlap of 12 mm (½ in) at the front edge. They should now be flush at the rear edge.

7 Assemble the building against the platform and drill through the lower part of the arch panel into the rear platform support. Fit quick-detach dowels into the latter as seen in Fig. 13.10, which also shows the top dowels.

Fig. 13.10

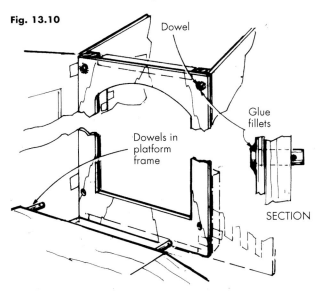

Unlike the standard arrangement, these dowels are supported by a glue fillet outside (see the small section). Note also how the support strips meet the strips that are on the partition and right side panel, and through which the dowels pass.

8 Take the lengths from the canopy panel and mark out the three valance pieces for it as shown in Fig. 13.11. Cut them out with the jigsaw and smooth the edges.

Fig. 13.11

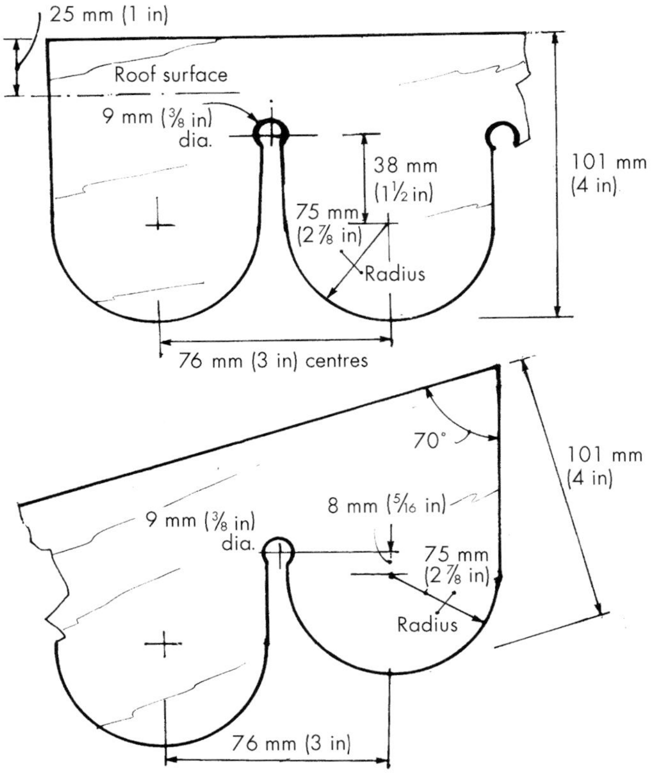

25 mm (1 in)
Roof surface
9 mm (⅜ in) dia.
38 mm (1½ in)
75 mm (2⅞ in)
Radius
101 mm (4 in)
76 mm (3 in) centres

70°
9 mm (⅜ in) dia.
8 mm (⁵⁄₁₆ in)
75 mm (2⅞ in)
Radius
101 mm (4 in)
76 mm (3 in)

9 Lay out the three roof panels, smallest in the centre. The largest is the canopy. Hinge these together as shown in Fig. 13.12 using the webbing as before. Allow the canopy piece to project equally each end.

Fig. 13.12

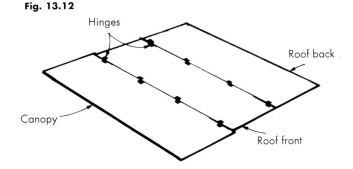

Hinges
Roof back
Canopy
Roof front

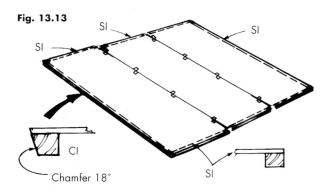

Fig. 13.13

SI · SI · SI · SI · SI
CI
Chamfer 18°

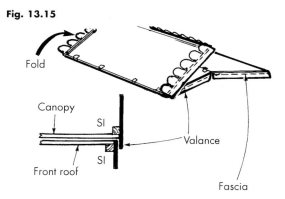

Fig. 13.15

Fold
Canopy
SI
Front roof
SI
Valance
Fascia

10 Plane an 18 degree chamfer in one strip of 12 × 12 mm (½ in) pine and glue and pin it under the front edge of the canopy panel, as shown in Fig. 13.13. Glue and pin the remaining strips of 12 × 12 (½ in) pine under the remaining edges of the assembly; leave a small gap between the ends of those at the ends of the roof proper, so that it can fold to form a pitched roof over the building.

11 Prop the canopy up on packing so that the edge strips are uppermost. Place a heavy supporting strip of wood against the edge strip as shown in Fig. 13.14, then glue and pin the front valance strip in place. Follow with the end valance strips and glue short pieces of 12 × 12 mm (½ in) pine in the corners where they meet the front valance. Also glue and pin 51 mm (2 in)-wide strips of plywood to the gable ends of the roof panels, as shown in Fig. 13.15. Note that they clear the valance when the canopy is folded back for storage. The roof panels stay flat in this condition.

Fig. 13.14

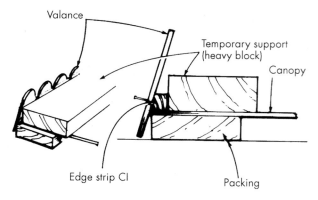

Valance
Temporary support (heavy block)
Canopy
Edge strip CI
Packing

12 The two seats (one for the waiting-room and the other for the station staff) are in 4 mm (³⁄₁₆ in) plywood, with 12 × 51 mm (½ × 2 in) pine support rails front and back and across the ends, as seen in Fig. 13.16. Glue and pin the end rails to the front and back ones, inset 4 mm (³⁄₁₆) in from the ends of the latter. This will allow you to make the end panels of the seats fit under the top of the seat. Notch them to go round the projecting ends of the front and back rails as shown. When properly glued up, the ends will be rigid. Further support will be gained when they are positioned next to the partition wall.

Fig. 13.16

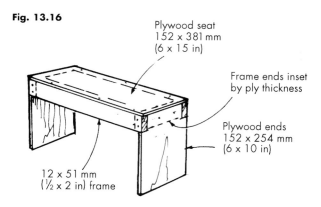

Plywood seat
152 × 381 mm
(6 x 15 in)
Frame ends inset by ply thickness
Plywood ends
152 × 254 mm
(6 x 10 in)
12 x 51 mm
(½ x 2 in) frame

13 Make the signal as shown in Fig. 13.17. The small panel behind the signal has a cut-out to allow light to show through either of the coloured acetate holes (red or green). You can use clear acetate, from a stationer, and colour it with felt pens.

The signal arm is the early type which goes down for 'clear'. Put small screws or nails into the

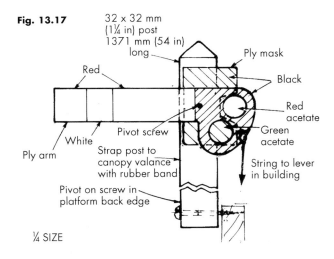

Fig. 13.17

32 x 32 mm (1¼ in) post 1371 mm (54 in) long

Ply mask

Black

Red acetate

Green acetate

String to lever in building

Red

White

Ply arm

Pivot screw

Strap post to canopy valance with rubber band

Pivot on screw in platform back edge

¼ SIZE

post to limit the movement of the arm to horizontal and down to 30 degrees. A piece of string holds it horizontal and has a loop which you pass through the wall, then through a screw eye, before you attach it to a lever inside. This is something you do while setting up the play-house for use, before you join the back wall to the side (see Fig. 13.18).

Fig. 13.18

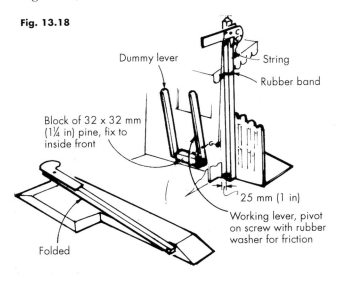

Dummy lever

String

Rubber band

Block of 32 x 32 mm (1¼ in) pine, fix to inside front

25 mm (1 in)

Folded

Working lever, pivot on screw with rubber washer for friction

The levers should be stiff to move, to prevent the signal resetting itself. Put a rubber washer between each lever and the strip of wood that supports it, before you insert the woodscrews on which they pivot.

The post folds back along the platform for storage, and is held steady with a rubber band over one of the lobes on the end valance, when set up for play.

14 The railway coach 'compartment' is shown in Fig. 13.19. You can cut the four gussets from the waste from the windows. Choose small wheels from a DIY or craft shop and add short strips of 32 × 32 mm (1¼ in) pine to the gussets so that the screws have support. Alternatively, you could fit small castors instead. The whole panel will be unstable unless you fix a couple of pieces of stone or other weights to the wheel supports. The users will be too busy pretending to be passengers to notice these external features. (You will need extra plywood and battens to make this optional accessory – see page 105.)

Fig. 13.19

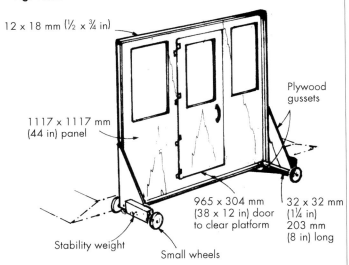

12 x 18 mm (½ x ¾ in)

Plywood gussets

1117 x 1117 mm (44 in) panel

965 x 304 mm (38 x 12 in) door to clear platform

32 x 32 mm (1¼ in) 203 mm (8 in) long

Stability weight

Small wheels

15 Back inside the building, the drum-shaped item represents a heating stove. It can be a plastic or cardboard container, or an oil drum. Decorate it to look convincing in its new role, and add a cardboard tube for a stove pipe. You can also fit a small shelf near the ticket window, for card train tickets.

Kitchen

This play-house represents a whole kitchen with dining area. The door can be the back door, or entry from the hall, or from another pretend room. Similarly, the service hatch may lead to the garden or to a pretend dining room.

Once inside, with the door closed against any full-scale household intrusions, domestic play is here in plenty, for the kitchen has L-shaped fitted units, shelves, work tops, a sink, a hob with a heat effect, and a washing machine that can wash and spin by use of a small handle. Furnishings include a table and bench seats that fold and nest to give extra space when cooking and laundry is the main theme. Accessories include a toaster with dummy toast, white on one side and brown on the other. (Just turn the toaster around before letting it pop up.) These crafty but comparatively easily made gadgets are all detailed.

The overall size is 1016 mm (40 in) square, 1270 mm (50 in) high at the front for the entrance down to 1143 mm (45 in) at the back, where headroom is not so important. In spite of the depth of the two work-tops, which are fixed to the walls, the whole assembly folds down to 482 mm (19 in) deep when stacked against the wall; see Fig. 14.1.

STAR RATING
Skill level ****
Cost *****
Child height *****

MATERIALS

6 mm (¼ in) plywood:
  half sheet 1219 ×
  1219 mm (48 in) or less
4 mm (³⁄₁₆ in) plywood: 3½
  sheets 2438 × 1219 mm
  (8 × 4 ft)
12 × 76 mm (½ × 3 in)
  pine: 3 at 1016 mm
  (40 in)
  7 at 228 mm (9 in)
18 × 44 mm (¾ × 1¾ in)
  pine: 127 mm (5 in)
32 × 32 mm (1¼ in) pine:
  76 mm (3 in)
12 × 18 mm (½ × ¾ in)
  pine: 3 at 1270 mm
  (50 in)
  4 at 1143 mm (45 in)
  5 at 1092 mm (43 in)
  20 at 1016 mm (40 in)
12 × 12 mm (½ × ½ in) pine:
  4 at 1016 mm (40 in)
Single wood slide channel
  section: 813 mm (32 in)
9 mm (⅜ in) dowel:
  203 mm (8 in)

6 mm (¼ in) dowel:
  162 mm (6 in)
2 mm (³⁄₃₂ in) clear styrene
  glazing: 406 × 152mm
  (16 × 6 in)
25 mm (1 in)-wide strong
  upholstery webbing:
  1828 mm (72 in)
Wire coat-hanger
6 flat small cupboard
  knobs
1 at 76 mm (3 in) flush
  hinge plus screws
2 pairs 38 mm (1½ in) butt
  hinges and screws
1 2 litre ice-cream
  container (rectangular)
20 mm (¾ in) panel pins
PVA glue
Glue sticks
Abrasive paper
Non-toxic paint
Velcro strip
Rubber bands
Thread

TOOLS

- Hand saw or hand-held
  circular saw
- Tenon saw
- Hand-held jigsaw
- Hammer
- Nail punch
- Drill
- Glue gun
- Domestic iron

- Screwdriver
- Sanding block or
  sander
- Stanley knife
- Pencil
- Rule
- Try square
- Paint brushes

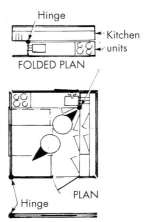

Hinge

Kitchen
units

FOLDED PLAN

PLAN

Hinge

1 Mark out the sheets of 4 mm (³⁄₁₆ in) plywood as shown in Fig. 14.2. Cut all the rectangular shapes with the hand-held circular saw or hand saw held at a low angle. Work on the floor, with a packing piece of 76 × 51 mm (3 × 2 in) timber underneath near the cutting line. Join up sawcuts at the door head by drilling to insert the jigsaw blade and cutting across. Drill opposite two corners of all cut-outs and use the jigsaw to make two cuts from each to the opposite (undrilled) corners. The floor is 813 mm (32 in) square from the half sheet. Stack all cut pieces flat on the floor until needed.

Fig. 14.1

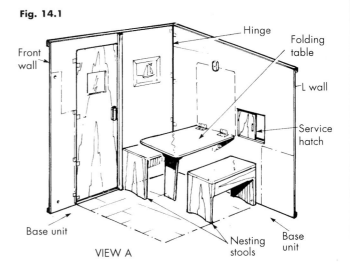

Front wall

Hinge

Folding table

L wall

Service hatch

Base unit

VIEW A

Nesting stools

Base unit

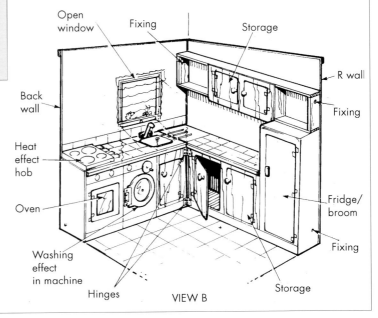

Open window

Fixing

Storage

R wall

Back wall

Fixing

Heat effect hob

Oven

Fridge/ broom

Fixing

Washing effect in machine

Hinges

Storage

VIEW B

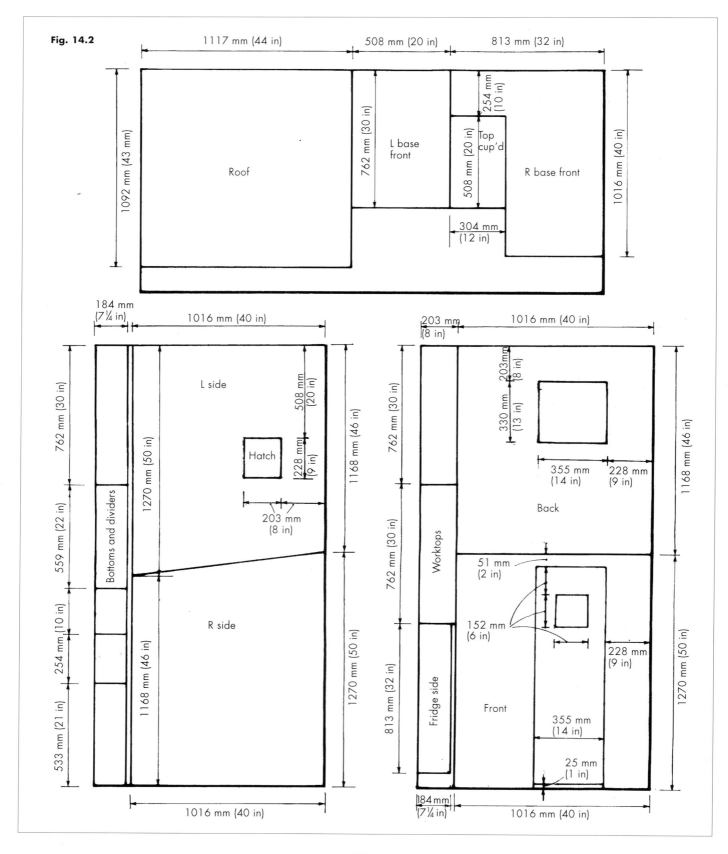

Fig. 14.2

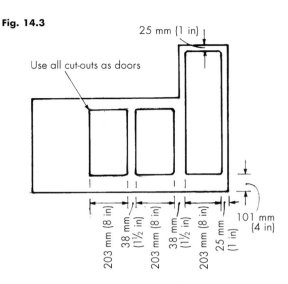

Fig. 14.3

Use all cut-outs as doors

25 mm (1 in)

101 mm (4 in)

203 mm (8 in)   38 mm (1½ in)   203 mm (8 in)   38 mm (1½ in)   203 mm (8 in)   25 mm (1 in)

2 Three of these panels are the cupboard fronts. Mark them out and cut the doors in the same way. Fig. 14.3 shows the main base unit, Fig. 14.4 is the sink/cooker base, and Fig. 14.5 is the eye-level cupboard. Stack these flat after cutting out all the openings and doors. Note the small radius at the

Fig. 14.4

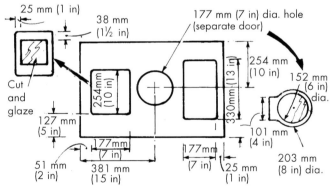

25 mm (1 in)

38 mm (1½ in)

177 mm (7 in) dia. hole (separate door)

254 mm (10 in)

152 mm (6 in) dia.

Cut and glaze

254mm (10 in)

330mm (13 in)

127 mm (5 in)

101 mm (4 in)

51 mm (2 in)   381 mm (15 in)   177mm (7 in)   177mm (7 in)   25 mm (1 in)   203 mm (8 in) dia.

Fig. 14.5

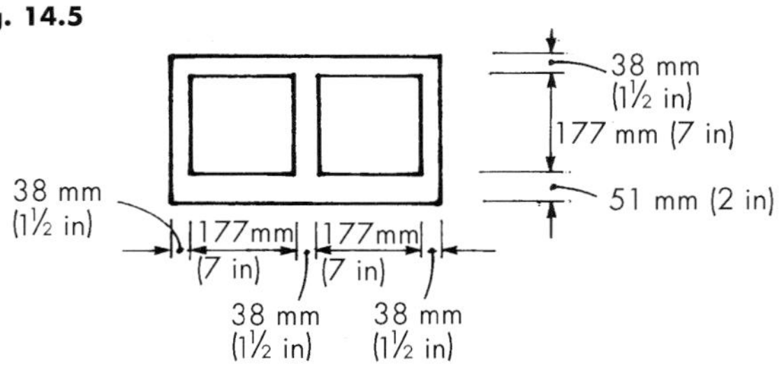

38 mm (1½ in)

38 mm (1½ in)   177 mm (7 in)   51 mm (2 in)

177mm (7 in)   177mm (7 in)   38 mm (1½ in)   38 mm (1½ in)

door corners, which is to avoid injury. Do not make these larger than 4 mm (3⁄16 in), or the design will not look up to date. Where you drilled corner holes for the jigsaw blade, two corners of each door will have a small quadrant missing, You can restore these by gluing in a very short slice of dowel, then sanding flush front and back.

3 Return to the two main front and left wall panels, shown in Fig. 14.6. At this stage you should fit all the webbing hinges, as described in Chapter 1. Note the arrangement of the webbing so as to get the hinges near the corners for maximum stability. Webbing hinges will have a less rigid action than metal hinges, but the doors fit flush in their panels and you can use small Velcro pads instead of catches.

Fig. 14.6

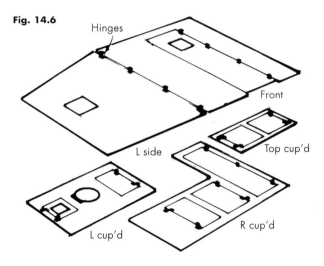

Hinges

Front

L side

Top cup'd

L cup'd

R cup'd

4 Glue and pin strips of 12 × 18 mm (½ × ¾ in) pine at the edges and door of the four main wall panels. Note from Fig. 14.7 which strips are on their edge and which are flat. Clench the points of any panel pins that protrude, knocking them sideways, in line with the grain, then forcing the points down below the surface with the nail punch.

Fig. 14.7

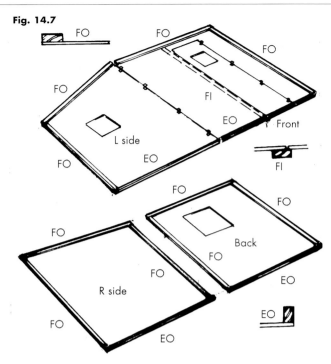

Fig. 14.9

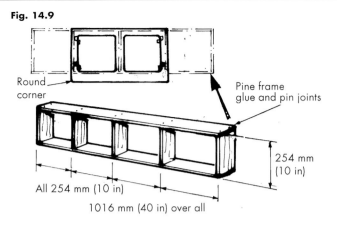

7 Using strips of 12 × 18 mm and 12 × 12 mm (½ × ¾ in, ½ × ½ in) pine, frame up the base unit comprising cupboards, work-top and fridge or broom cupboard, all as shown in Fig. 14.10. All joints need to be glued and pinned. Start by fixing the 12 × 18 mm (½ × ¾ in) edging strips to the work-top and bottom, then the 12 × 12 mm (½ in) cross strips to the dividing and end panels and the fridge/broom cupboard top. When the glue has set, clench any panel pin points flush, then assemble the components with more glue and pins,

5 Using the jigsaw, cut the fascia strip for the front of the roof as shown in Fig. 14.8, glue and pin strips of 12 × 18 mm (½ × ¾ in) to the roof panel as in the same figure, and glue and pin the fascia in place. The roof should fit to overhang the walls.

Fig. 14.8

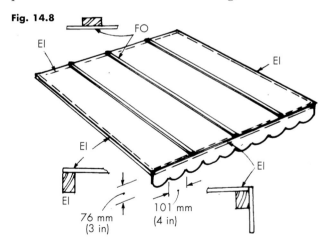

6 Make the box-like shelves and cupboard frame from 12 × 76 mm (½ × 3 in) pine (you can saw the tongue and groove edges from interior cladding strip for this). Fig. 14.9 shows the dimensions; all joints are simple butt type. Check for right angles with the try square, then glue and pin them. Glue and pin the cupboard front to the edge of the frame, flush at the top edge.

Fig. 14.10

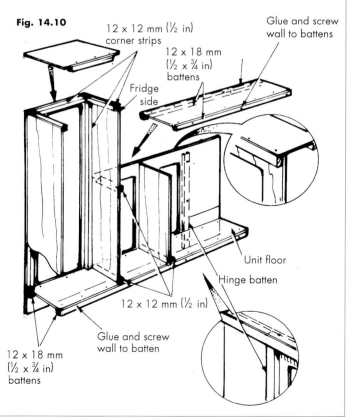

checking with the try square. Glue and pin the external vertical strip as seen in the detail. This will take the metal hinges joining the other base unit.

Lay the right wall panel on packing, level on the floor. Lay the finished base unit face down on the floor. Apply glue to the edges of the edge strips of the base unit then lower it onto the wall panel. Make sure that the bottom edge of the wall is in line with the bottom edge of the base unit by holding a strip of wood vertical against the two edges. When the glue is set, you can reinforce the joints with a few short screws or some panel pins from the outside face of the wall into the edge strips. Check thoroughly inside the cupboards to see that there are no sharp points protruding. Clench pin points or apply a blob of hot-melt glue to screw points to prevent injury.

8 Make the other base unit in a similar way, as in Fig. 14.11. Note the stepped floor to the oven part. Cut a hole in the work-top to fit the ice cream container which serves as a sink, leaving a 32 mm (1¼ in) space for the taps between the container edge lip (not the hole) and the back edge. Cut the washing machine door from the 4 mm (³⁄₁₆ in) plywood and use a flush hinge on its back face to fix it the the front of the cupboard panel. Do not fix the unit to the back wall yet.

9 Using the jigsaw on its slowest speed, or a fine-tooth pad saw, cut the circular glazing for the washing machine door from the styrene sheet.

Also cut the remainder of the sheet for the oven door. These are straight cuts, which you can make by scoring half through with the laminate cutting blade in a Stanley knife, then snapping off the waste. Use blobs of hot-melt glue to fix the glazing to the inner faces of the doors.

10 The washing machine wash/spin effect comes next, and is detailed in Fig. 14.12. You can gain access to the rear of the door by opening it, and to the inside of the machine panel from the back.

First glue three short pieces of 12 × 12 mm (½ in) pine to the back of the door against the glazing edge. These are spacers for a rear cover, which you cut from 4 mm (³⁄₁₆ in) plywood, drilling the centre

Fig. 14.11

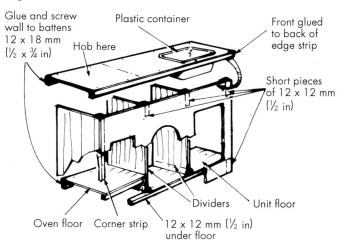

Glue and screw wall to battens 12 x 18 mm (½ x ¾ in)
Hob here
Plastic container
Front glued to back of edge strip
Short pieces of 12 x 12 mm (½ in)
Oven floor   Corner strip   12 x 12 mm (½ in) under floor
Dividers   Unit floor

Fig. 14.12

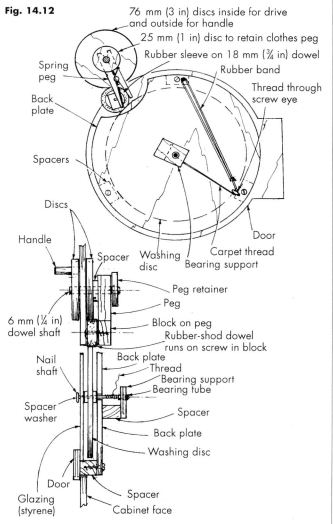

76 mm (3 in) discs inside for drive and outside for handle
25 mm (1 in) disc to retain clothes peg
Rubber sleeve on 18 mm (¾ in) dowel
Rubber band
Thread through screw eye
Spring peg
Back plate
Spacers
Discs
Handle
Door
Carpet thread
Bearing support
Peg retainer
Peg
6 mm (¼ in) dowel shaft
Washing disc
Block on peg
Rubber-shod dowel runs on screw in block
Nail shaft
Back plate
Thread
Bearing support
Bearing tube
Spacer washer
Spacer
Back plate
Washing disc
Door
Spacer
Glazing (styrene)
Cabinet face

using a 6 mm (¼ in) bit, and the edge to take fixing screws. Drill the centre of the glazing to take a 38 mm (1½ in) wire nail. It has to turn smoothly, without slop, in the hole. This will be the axle for a disk of 4 mm (³⁄₁₆ in) plywood, which represents the washing. Paint this white, plus some odd coloured shapes and grey spots, to look like bubbles. Drill it centrally for a tight fit on the nail. Make a small spacer from thinner plywood or use thick small metal washers or a little nut, to prevent it rubbing on the glazing.

Push the nail through the glazing from the front, through the spacer and fix the nail in the disk with hot-melt glue while you hold the nail straight. It has to be at right angles to the disk so that it will spin with wobbling when the rear bearing is in place. Screw the back cover to the spacers. The hole should clear the nail axle. The bearing is a small piece of metal or nylon tube (a slice from a used ball pen ink tube may fit). Fix it with the glue gun in a scrap of plywood on a short 12 × 18 mm (½ × ¾ in) spacer. Slide this around on the back cover while the axle is in the tube. Stop when the disk spins freely without touching the glazing. If there is pronounced wobble, remove the cover and refix the axle by melting the glue again with the gun, until all is well.

Glue one end of a piece of thread to the axle, wind it round the axle and attach the other end via a strong rubber band to the bearing support, after passing the thread through a screw eye as detailed. When the disk has been turned several times, the band is stretched and spins the disk back again. You now have a spin effect. The wash cycle is contrived by turning a handle, as you will see from

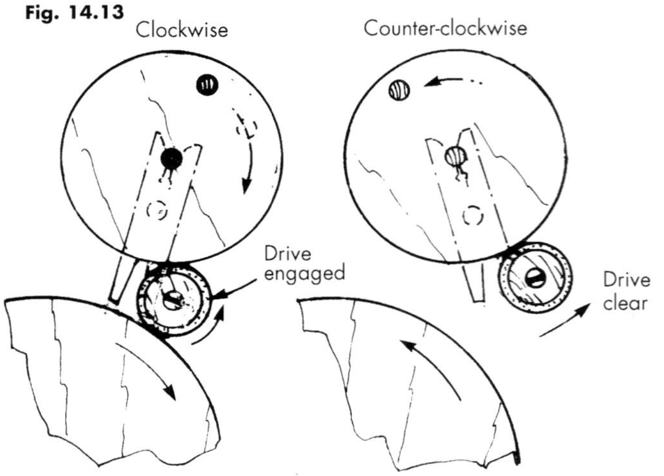

Fig. 14.13. In order to get 'spin', the friction drive has to be disengaged. An intermediate idler roller is mounted on a spring-type clothes peg on the dowel that carries the winding and drive disks. All the details are shown in the diagrams.

When the handle is turned clockwise, the peg moves the intermediate roller onto the washing disc, which is then also turned clockwise until the rubber band is fully stretched, then the drive skids. Turn the handle a small amount counter-clockwise, and the peg will pull the idler out of contact, allowing the washing to spin backwards also in a counter-clockwise direction.

11 The hob heating effect is similar to that used in the camper project, but has four hobs. Fig. 14.14 shows the details. Leave space between the front and rear hobs so that plywood panels can pass unseen underneath. Draw the circles then cut parallel slots between, having equal-width spaces between. Support the panel on spacing strips just thick enough to allow four 'heat' panels to move. Cut these to fit together as shown and equip each with a small dowel slice to form slide handles. Paint these panels red. Then with them all under the top panel and pushed to the right, spray black paint through the hob slots. The 'heat' panels will now appear to be turned off. When dry, each panel

Fig. 14.13

Clockwise Counter-clockwise

Drive engaged

Drive clear

Fig. 14.14

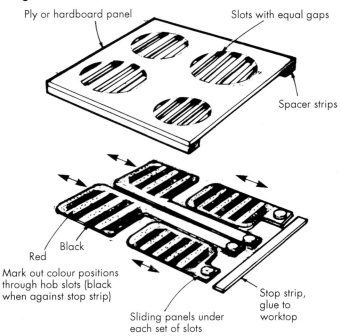

Ply or hardboard panel
Slots with equal gaps
Spacer strips
Red Black
Mark out colour positions through hob slots (black when against stop strip)
Sliding panels under each set of slots
Stop strip, glue to worktop

will show red 'hot' when its handle is slid to the left against a stop strip on the work top. Individual hobs can now be turned on to show low or full heat. Paint the area of the panel around the hobs a contrasting colour.

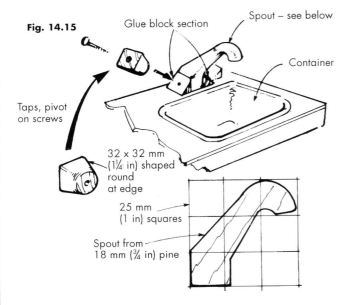

Fig. 14.15

Glue block section

Spout – see below

Container

Taps, pivot on screws

32 × 32 mm (1¼ in) shaped round at edge

25 mm (1 in) squares

Spout from 18 mm (¾ in) pine

12 Make the tap unit from an offcut of 18 mm (¾ in) pine, shown gridded in Fig. 14.15. Use triangular glue block pieces to mount the taps each side. The taps are slices of 32 mm (1¼ in) square pine. Shave these to a round shape at their bottom edge and drill them to pivot on woodscrews. Glue the whole unit behind the sink.

You can paint the work-tops gloss and rule them to represent tiles, using a Tipp-Ex pen, then clear varnish over. Fix the base unit to the back wall as you did earlier.

13 Glue the vertical strip of 12 × 18 mm (½ × ¾ in) pine to the front of the base unit when both walls are pulled together at the corner, then fit the hinges as shown in Fig. 14.16. The two work-tops should now form a smooth L-shape near the sink and the rear wall should be against the end of the shelf unit. Drill a 9 mm (⅜ in) hole through the back edge strip here into the shelf end upright, and after opening out the hole in the wall, glue a dowel into the shelf part as a register and support. When the walls are folded for storage, the work-top units will hinge close together. Erect the other two walls and with the right and back walls

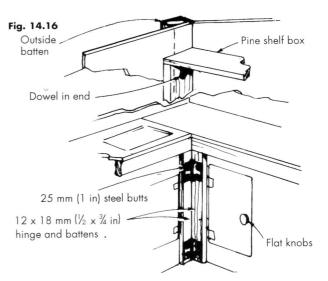

Fig. 14.16

Outside batten

Pine shelf box

Dowel in end

25 mm (1 in) steel butts

12 × 18 mm (½ × ¾ in) hinge and battens .

Flat knobs

open again, bring the joining corners together. Drill through the facing uprights 76 mm (3 in) from top and bottom, open out the holes and fit dowels as before. The lower dowel of the left side goes into the end of the cooker, and those on the front wall go into the fridge and shelf end. The roof will keep the top edges of the walls square. It just rests over them, but if you have the play-house outdoors in windy weather, strap the roof down at each corner with strong rubber bands.

14 Use the piece of plywood that you cut from the service hatch opening as a sliding door, gluing strips of channel to the outside of the wall to carry it. Add a small piece of 12 × 12 mm (½ in) pine for a handle inside and outside, and to stop the door running right out. Fig. 14.17 shows the

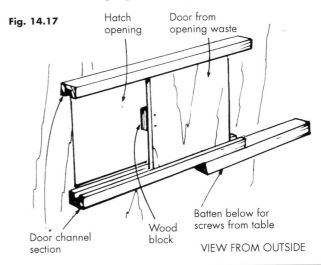

Fig. 14.17

Hatch opening

Door from opening waste

Door channel section

Wood block

Batten below for screws from table

VIEW FROM OUTSIDE

detail, and the extra strip of 12 × 18 mm (½ × ¾ in) pine which you glue outside to take the hinge screws from the folding table.

15 Cut the 6 mm (¼ in) ply for the floor to 813 mm (32 in) square to complete the main work. You can now make the table, shown in Fig. 14.18, from 6 mm (¼ in) plywood and fit a strip of 12 × 18 mm (½ × ¾ in) pine underneath to take the hinge screws. The leg is also the same plywood and includes a webbing hinged flap which you glue underneath. You may like to glue two small pieces of 12 × 18 mm (½ × ¾ in) pine to the floor panel to prevent the leg from being kicked askew. Put a turn-button on the wall to hold the table up.

Fig. 14.18

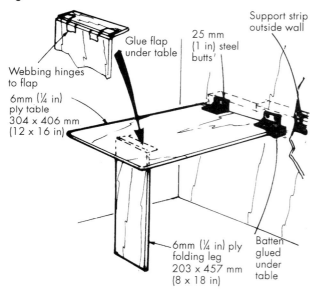

Webbing hinges to flap

Glue flap under table

25 mm (1 in) steel butts'

Support strip outside wall

6mm (¼ in) ply table 304 x 406 mm (12 x 16 in)

6mm (¼ in) ply folding leg 203 x 457 mm (8 x 18 in)

Batten glued under table

16 The seats are designed to fit inside each other for storage, or when more space is needed in the kitchen, so note the dimensions in Fig. 14.19. Rigidity is given by the 12 × 76 mm (½ × 3 in) pine rail at the back of each seat, and the 12 × 12 mm (½ in) pine strips glued and pinned in the ends. Adjust the height of the seats to suit.

Fig. 14.19

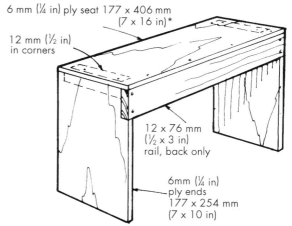

6 mm (¼ in) ply seat 177 x 406 mm (7 x 16 in)*

12 mm (½ in) in corners

12 x 76 mm (½ x 3 in) rail, back only

6mm (¼ in) ply ends 177 x 254 mm (7 x 10 in)

* Note: make other seat 381 mm (15 in) long

17 The toaster (Fig. 14.20) is some more trickery. Make it from pieces of 12 × 76 mm (½ × 3 in) and 12 × 18 mm (½ × ¾ in), plus a piece of coat-hanger wire which a rubber band lifts to eject the plywood 'toast'.

Fig. 14.20

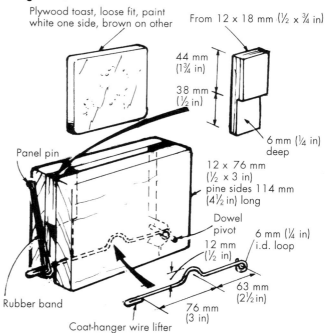

Plywood toast, loose fit, paint white one side, brown on other

From 12 x 18 mm (½ x ¾ in)

44 mm (1¾ in)

38 mm (½ in)

6 mm (¼ in) deep

Panel pin

12 x 76 mm (½ x 3 in) pine sides 114 mm (4½ in) long

Dowel pivot

6 mm (¼ in) i.d. loop

12 mm (½ in)

63 mm (2½ in)

Rubber band

76 mm (3 in)

Coat-hanger wire lifter

Indoor Tree-House

Some of the other projects can be taken outside in fine weather; this one is intended to be used only indoors, in the corner of a room or garage. In fact here is a play-house especially for homes without gardens. Of wardrobe-like proportions, it is a split-level enclosure with external and internal access. The front wall panel is styled to give the effect of trunk and leaves, with doors incorporated. Children climb a short distance using footholds cut in the plywood surface and grab handles disguised as stumpy branches. There is an internal hatchway and a pop-up roof light cum spyhole. Underneath the lower floor there is a crawl space with a store cupboard among the roots. Designed for the younger age group, there is space for four in the two main compartments; one older child can curl up in each. Although the construction allows it to be folded up, it may be more convenient to leave it assembled. A firm fixing is needed to steady it against the wall, such as a large screw in a plug, or a toggle bolt. Compared with a well-built wardrobe it is not heavy, but when children start swarming up the outside and bouncing inside, it would be wise to resist their efforts to topple it over.

The views in Fig. 15.1 are the suggested treatment, but there is scope for non-structural design variations by its intended inhabitants.

STAR RATING
Skill level ****
Cost ****
Child height * ¯ ***

MATERIALS

6 mm (¼ in) plywood:
    1 sheet 2438 ×
    1219 mm (8 × 4 ft)
4 mm (³⁄₁₆ in) plywood:
    2 sheets 2438 ×
    1219 mm (8 × 4 ft)
18 × 44 mm (¾ × 1¾ in)
    pine: 304 mm (12 in)
12 ×18 mm (½ × ¾ in)
    pine: 2 at 965 mm
    (38 in)
    7 at 660 mm (26 in)
    10 at 508 mm (20 in)
12 ×12 mm (½ in) pine:
    4 at 508 mm (20 in)
9 mm (⅜ in) dowel:
    355 mm (14 in)

6 mm (¼ in) dowel:
    152 mm (6 in)
25 mm (1 in)-wide strong
    upholstery webbing:
    2540 mm (100 in)
4 steel bolts 4 × 40 mm
    (³⁄₁₆ × 1½ in) with wing
    nuts and washers
1 no.12 76 mm (3 in)
    screw and wall plug
PVA glue
Glue sticks
Panel pins
Abrasive paper
Non-toxic paint
Hook and loop strip

TOOLS

- Hand saw
- Tenon saw
- Hand-held jigsaw
- Drill
- Screwdriver
- Hammer
- Nail punch
- Scissors
- Glue gun
- Domestic iron
- Paint brushes
- Pencil
- Rule
- Compass
- Try square

–Fig. 15.1

Folding table
Seat
Roof hatch
Floor
Storage
Footholds Floor hatch

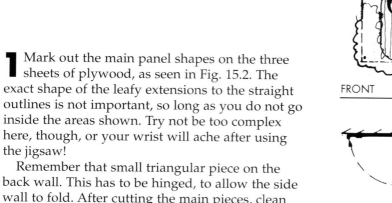

Ceiling of room
Room wall
FRONT
Hinge against wall
FOLDED PLAN

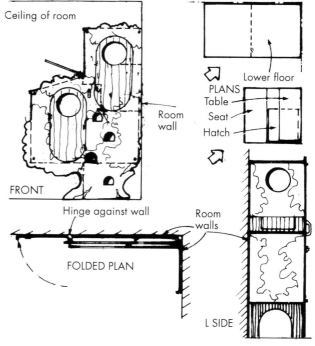

Lower floor
PLANS
Table
Seat
Hatch
Room walls
L SIDE

1 Mark out the main panel shapes on the three sheets of plywood, as seen in Fig. 15.2. The exact shape of the leafy extensions to the straight outlines is not important, so long as you do not go inside the areas shown. Try not be too complex here, though, or your wrist will ache after using the jigsaw!

Remember that small triangular piece on the back wall. This has to be hinged, to allow the side wall to fold. After cutting the main pieces, clean up the edges with abrasive paper, and lay them flat until needed.

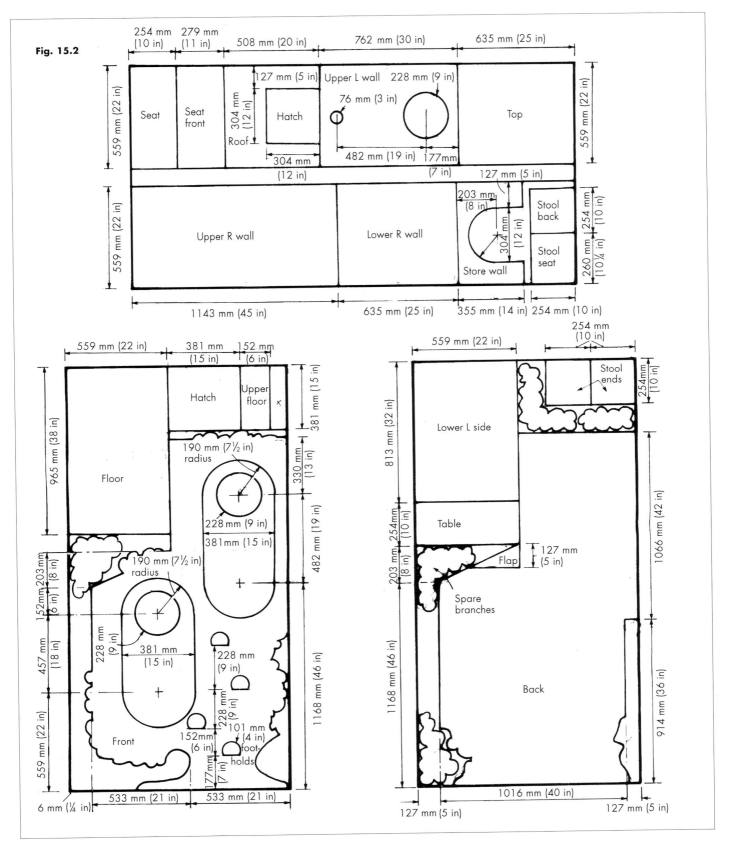

Fig. 15.2

Fig. 15.3

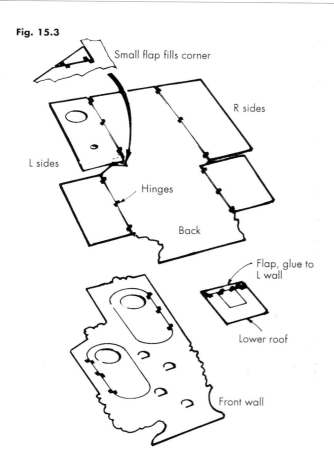

Small flap fills corner

R sides

L sides

Hinges

Back

Flap, glue to L wall

Lower roof

Front wall

Fig. 15.4

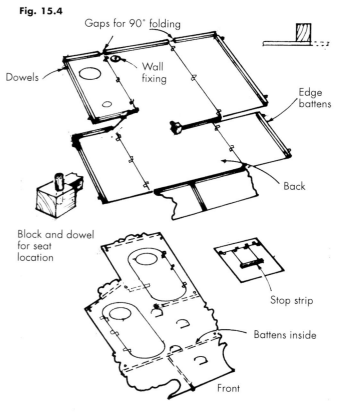

Gaps for 90° folding

Dowels

Wall fixing

Edge battens

Back

Block and dowel for seat location

Stop strip

Battens inside

Front

2 Following Fig. 15.3, hinge the panels together and hang the doors and roof hatch. The hinging technique is explained in Chapter 1 and in most of the other projects. Make a sound job of those door hinges. If your children are well-rounded and gymnastic, it might be a good idea to try one door for its reaction to their antics, before hinging the second one in the same way. Alternatively you could opt for small steel hinges in the first place, in which case use short screws and add a plywood patch behind to accommodate sufficient length without the points protruding.

3 Glue and pin the battens to the panels where shown in Fig. 15.4. Allow a gap at the top pieces so that the side walls can swing out. You will also need a small block drilled for a dowel, as shown on the back wall. This is for supporting and locating the seat and small piece of floor at level two. The dowel has to project 18 mm (¾ in) to go through a batten on the seat and the plywood floor

piece. Note which battens are edge-mounted and which lie flat. Clench over any projecting points of panel pins, and slightly round the ends of the dowel to allow easy entry.

4 Make up the seat for level two with plywood panels and battens, as shown in Fig. 15.5. Note that the gussets go on the inside of the battens, and that the bottom batten projects far enough to pass through a hole in the front wall and has a hole for a 9 mm (⅜ in) dowel which will lock it in place there. The hole at the other end has to fit over the dowel mentioned in step 3. This batten supports the front of the seat. The seat leans against the upper left side wall and rests on the batten there. Round off the front edge and nearest corner of the seat, as it projects near the doorway slightly. When you assemble the tree house for use, the seat helps to steady the front wall while you secure the corners with the dowel and pin method already described in the other projects.

Fig. 15.5

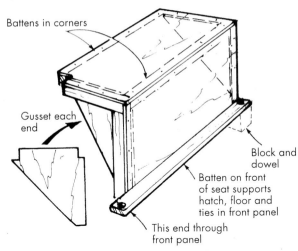

Battens in corners

Gusset each end

Block and dowel

Batten on front of seat supports hatch, floor and ties in front panel

This end through front panel

5 Glue and pin a pair of battens under the floor of level one and locate the store wall, which will support the floor while it is fitted. Drill the floor for its fixings. Go close to its edges, so that the holes can be drilled through into the supporting battens. To do this in comfort, lay the back wall on the floor, drill the back holes, then lean the front wall upright away from the scene and transfer the floor and store wall to it, before you drill the front holes. The holes are 6 mm (¼ in) for the centre four and corresponding dowels in the battens. Those in each corner are to take the 4 mm (³⁄₁₆ in) bolts (Fig. 15.6).

Fig. 15.6

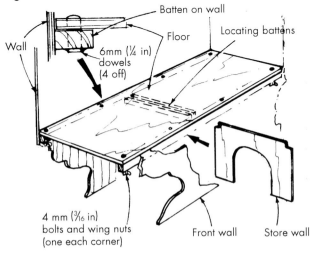

Wall

Batten on wall

Floor

Locating battens

6mm (¼ in) dowels (4 off)

4 mm (³⁄₁₆ in) bolts and wing nuts (one each corner)

Front wall

Store wall

For a trial run, prop or screw the back wall to the room wall where it will be used. When you assemble the floor to the walls, position the store wall and fit the bolts to the rear holes while you can easily reach them. Then with the front wall loosely in position, push the floor over the dowels in the front batten, secure the top of the wall to the side walls via the quick-detach dowel fittings (described on earlier projects) and bolt the front two corners of the floor. This is a trial assembly, because you now have to do more work inside, and access is easier without the front in place.

6 Make the floor hatch for level two from more 6 mm (¼ in) plywood. Hinge it to a narrow plywood flap, which you now glue to the right side wall so that the hatch rests on the wall batten when closed. Thus the hinges only support the hatch when it is opened. The batten just mentioned will also support the fixed piece of floor, as shown in Fig. 15.7 – you need a small extra piece of batten to support a dowel which will go through a hole in the fixed floor. The other corner of the floor goes over the dowel that protrudes through the seat batten and is also shown in Fig. 15.7. The seat batten, you remember, supports the hatch when closed. Children can use the footholds to climb up inside, to reach the seat.

Fig. 15.7

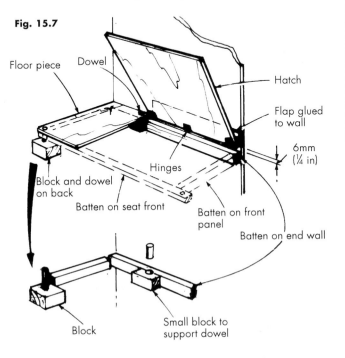

Floor piece

Dowel

Hatch

Flap glued to wall

6mm (¼ in)

Hinges

Block and dowel on back

Batten on seat front

Batten on front panel

Batten on end wall

Block

Small block to support dowel

7 Make the folding table from the 4 mm (³⁄₁₆ in) plywood (size shown in Fig. 15.2). Hinge a flap to the side edge and glue it to the right wall above the open hatch. Make the folding bracket and secure it under the table top in the same way as seen in Fig. 15.8. The table rests on a batten on the back wall and you can hold it in the folded position with a small piece of Velcro strip.

Fig. 15.8

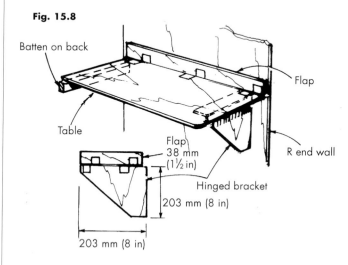

Batten on back
Table
Flap
Flap
38 mm (1½ in)
203 mm (8 in)
203 mm (8 in)
Hinged bracket
R end wall

8 The two roof panels sit on the top battens of the walls between the overlapping leaf parts of the walls and the room walls. Fit small pieces of Velcro strip to secure them. You can prize them free with a screwdriver near the strip pieces whenever you need to fold the project for storage.

9 Ideally, the tree-house should be sited in a room corner, so position the back wall and upper right side wall in there, corner in corner as it were. If the room has a thick skirting, add packing behind the back wall panel above it where you

Fig. 15.9

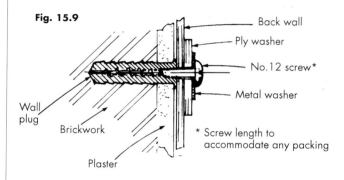

Back wall
Ply washer
No.12 screw*
Metal washer
Wall plug
Brickwork
Plaster
* Screw length to accommodate any packing

intend to make a fixing to the room wall. This detail is shown in Fig. 15.9. This is important, because children climbing up the front wall will cause it to wobble and might tip it over, as they might a bookcase or a narrow bunk bed. Do make sure that the wall to which you fix it is not a flimsy partition, and that the fixing is secure. That shown in the diagram is suitable for brick or strong block walls.

10 You may feel that hand grips would augment the footholds for small children, who can also grab the edges of the foothold above. Fig. 15.10 shows an example which you screw in place vertically, with screws from inside the front wall right through into the 12 × 18 mm (½ × ¾ in) strip.

Fig. 15.10

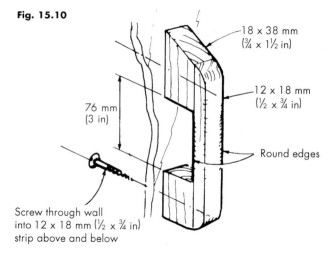

18 × 38 mm (¾ × 1½ in)
12 × 18 mm (½ × ¾ in)
Round edges
76 mm (3 in)
Screw through wall into 12 × 18 mm (½ × ¾ in) strip above and below

11 The floor of level one looks unfurnished, so make the stool shown in Fig. 15.11. It has one side open so that small items may be stowed inside, The construction is from 4 mm (³⁄₁₆ in) plywood with 12 × 12 mm (½ in) strips glued and pinned in the corners. Clench any panel pin points over flush inside to avoid scratches and sand all the edges and corners to a rounded shape.

12 Sand all rough uneven or sharp areas smooth, and paint the inside of the tree-house light bright colours. Clear varnish the outside of the doors and paint the leafy parts mottled green. You can outline individual leaves for better effect, and paint the trunk areas a streaky brown

Fig. 15.11

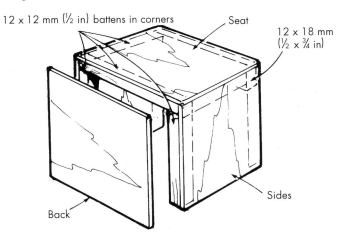

12 x 12 mm (½ in) battens in corners

Seat

12 x 18 mm (½ x ¾ in)

Back

Sides

with interesting details; make the footholds look like broken hollow branches and woodpecker holes.

Although this project is not designed primarily for use outdoors, you might use weatherproof paint, fix it to an outside wall and protect it in winter with polythene sheeting. The exposed joints at the corners and roof may be taped over with horticultural tape, but use hook and loop tape patches to form door 'catches' and plug the openings with the plywood waste which you cut from them, and from the footholds.

TIP: BATTEN JIG

When fixing the inset battens that form part of the quick-detach corner joint of a wall, the outside edge of the batten has to be positioned to accommodate the thickness of one batten, which is 12 mm (½ in), plus the thickness of a piece of plywood. Thus you can make a spacing jig from these materials and use it to check and position the batten that you will be fixing. Move it along the edge after you have pinned one end of the batten.

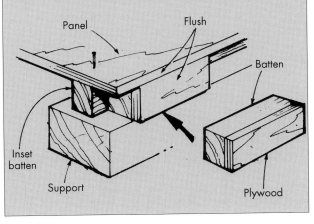

Panel

Flush

Batten

Inset batten

Support

Plywood

TIP: THIRD HAND

There comes a time when you have no spare hands to hold a panel pin – for example, when assembling a corner and you need one hand to hold a support behind the joint, and the other to hold the hammer. Put a blob of modelling clay (Plasticene) where the panel pin is to go, then push the pin into it. Hit the panel pin once to get it through the plywood and start it in the batten, then remove the clay and finish the hammer work.

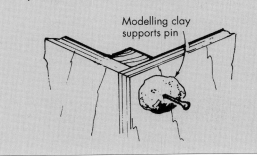

Modelling clay supports pin

Index